A FRENCH TRAGEDY

Contemporary French Culture and Society

edited by Richard J. Golsan,
Mary Jean Green, and Lynn A. Higgins

Tzvetan Todorov

A FRENCH
TRAGEDY

Scenes of Civil War,
Summer 1944

Translated by Mary Byrd Kelly

Translation edited and annotated by
Richard J. Golsan

DARTMOUTH COLLEGE

Published by University Press of New England
Hanover and London

DARTMOUTH COLLEGE

Published by University Press of New England, Hanover, NH 03755

© 1996 by the Trustees of Dartmouth College

Originally published in French as *Une Tragédie française — Été 44: Scènes de guerre civile.* Copyright © Editions du Sevil, 1994.

Printed in the United States of America

5 4 3 2 1

Library of Congress Cataloging-in-Publication Data

Todorov, Tzvetan, 1939–
 [Tragédie française. English]
 A French tragedy : scenes of civil war, summer 1944 / by Tzvetan
Todorov ; translated by Mary Byrd Kelly ; translation edited and
annotated by Richard J. Golsan.
  p. cm. — (Contemporary French culture and society)
 Includes bibliographical references.
 ISBN 0–87451–747–8
 1. World War, 1939–1945 — France — Saint-Amand-Mont-Rond. 2. Saint-
Amand-Mont-Rond (France) — History. 3. Sadrin, René. 4. Mayors —
France — Saint-Amand-Mont-Rond — Biography. 5. World War, 1939–1945 —
Personal narratives, French. I. Title. II. Series.
 D802.F82S21496813   1996
 940.54'8144552 — dc20   96–11603
 ⊚

CONTENTS

PREFACE TO THE
ENGLISH EDITION

The original edition of A *French Tragedy* was intended for French readers familiar with the context surrounding the dramatic events related in the book. It might therefore be helpful to recall some of the elements of that context here.

After the German army's lightening-quick victory in 1940, France signed an armistice agreement and immediately took its first steps on the road to collaboration. The head of state, Marshal Philippe Pétain, and his cabinet ministers, the most influential of whom was Pierre Laval, chose to lead the French State while at the same time agreeing to follow orders from Berlin or from the German embassy in Paris. They claimed that in so doing they spared the French people the consequences of direct occupation, but in fact they accomplished everything the Germans wanted and more. France provided Germany with all the raw materials it asked for, along with labor for its industries and, most serious of all, with Jews destined for death.

Facing this collaborationist France stood another France, a fighting France, the France of the Resistance. Its beginnings were difficult: Charles de Gaulle's call to resistance, broadcast from London on June 18, 1940, went largely unnoticed, and de Gaulle himself had great difficulty establishing himself as sole French interlocutor with the heads of the Allied Forces in Britain and the United States. Interior resistance was equally slow to get started: in 1940 the Communists, who in principle were active enemies of Hitler, were paralyzed by the German-Russian nonaggression pact; it was not until 1941 and the invasion of Russia that they could clearly identify their adversary. Other events, however, reinforced resistance: the German army's invasion of the Southern Zone of France in 1942, the Allies' military successes in 1942–43, and the Service du Travail Obligatoire (or STO, the Forced Work Service) instituted in 1943, which forced young Frenchmen to go to Germany. By 1944, resistance was effervescing; after the Normandy invasion of June 6, it was everywhere.

The political situation of wartime France is sometimes hard to understand, for it was a result of the superposition of two distinct conflicts. One was the conflict between France and Germany; the other, within France itself, was between the political right and left. Of course, this superposition was only partial. The ideological debate between the right and left, a conflict that was exacerbated in the wake of the victory of the Popular Front in 1936, continued to fuel debates during the Occupation. The French right, especially its most extremist elements, may indeed have felt regret over the defeat of France; but at the same time, the right rejoiced over the defeat of the left or what in this case amounted to the same thing, the Republic. Pétain therefore pursued a program of "national revolution," and the slogan "Work, Family, Fatherland" replaced the republican trinity of "Liberty, Equality, Fraternity." Within this extreme right were two rival tendencies: one more conservative and nationalist, the other more revolutionary and ideological (Fascist).

Very soon the Vichy authorities felt obliged to assemble a paramilitary force intended for armed combat within the country, against any and all political or military enemies. Its first stage would be the Service d'ordre légionnaire, transformed into the *milice*, or militia, in early 1943.[1] It was this body, the militia, that

---

1. A combination of totalitarian political party and private police force, the militia was created by Pierre Laval in January 1943 to combat France's "internal enemies"—Communists, Jews, and Resistance fighters. The organization was also created to serve as a political counterweight to ultracollaborationists, such as Jacques Doriot and his Parti populaire français, whom Laval considered rivals for power. Although Laval was the titular head of

was responsible for the worst exactions committed during the Occupation: denunciations, tortures, rapes, murders. The Resistance and the militia fought an open war. France was thus not only the stage for a Franco-German war; it was also the stage, particularly in 1943–44, for a Franco-French civil war.

It is an episode from this war between militiamen and Resistance fighters, with the civilian population often cast in the role of hostage, that is the subject of this book. The episode took place during the summer of 1944, between D-Day and the Liberation. On June 6, 1944, the resisters took over Saint-Amand Montrond, a town in central France, believing that the Liberation would follow immediately. Shortly afterward they withdrew, but a fatal chain reaction was set off by their initial action, an action followed by a series of tragic events, illustrating in an exemplary manner the complexities of the political and military situation of France in those troubled times.

The relationship between the postwar French and the Vichy episode has undergone a complex evolution, analyzed in particular by Henry Rousso (*The Vichy Syndrome*, 1991, and in collaboration with E. Conan, *Vichy, un passé qui ne passe pas*, 1944). One after another, four legends—one Vichy's own, another one Communist, still another Gaullist, and a fourth defeatist—arose, competed against each other, refined their differences with further distinctions, and became more nuanced. It should be added that, contrary to what is sometimes asserted, the purge that immediately followed the war was not insignificant; but one cannot entirely "purge" a population that, as a whole, accepted its fate. (We are well aware of this today in the aftermath of the fall of Communist regimes in Eastern Europe: to survive, each and every person had to "collaborate," though to varying degrees.)

---

the militia, its commander was Joseph Darnand, a decorated World War I veteran and extreme right-wing militant who had run a trucking company between the wars. The most detailed account in English of the militia, its origins, leaders, and activities, can be found in Bertram Gordon, *Collaborationism in France during the Second World War* (Ithaca, N.Y.: Cornell University Press, 1980), 166–95.

The debates surrounding the interpretation of this page of history are still going on, and some are among the hottest in France today, a fact that reveals a significant facet of late-twentieth-century France and perhaps other European countries as well. One no longer encounters the slightest difficulty in denouncing any particular turpitude of the Vichy regime. On the other hand, it is not nearly so easy to remain dispassionate when analyzing the action taken by the Resistance for the Free French forces (in London or Algiers). Associations of former Resistance members, veterans, or deportees see to it that the official image of the past remains unchanged, and the moral authority enjoyed by former heroes and victims cuts short many a debate, particularly if it takes place in the public sphere (that is, in the mass media, especially television) rather than in the specialized publications of historians. It is only natural that the interpretation of the past should serve the present, but that does not mean that we can allow any one particular interpretation to be made sacred and be transformed into a pious image. The historian cannot let himself be led by any principle other than the search for truth, even if he knows that there is no such thing as absolute truth in this world.

Aside from the reactions of former participants—who, by force of circumstances, are becoming fewer and fewer—two types of attitudes toward Vichy are the most prevalent today: vindication by trivialization, and virtuous indignation. Illustrations of the first are found in the judgment rendered in the initial court proceedings concerning Paul Touvier, the former militiaman accused of crimes against humanity; the case was dismissed on the grounds that France during the Occupation was not a totalitarian state.[2] The same attitude is present in the obstacles placed on the path

2. Paul Touvier, head of the Second Section (intelligence) of the *militia* in Lyons, was responsible for a number of crimes, including theft and murder, during the Occupation. Following the war, Touvier went into hiding and, with the help of members of the Catholic clergy, secured a pardon for his wartime activities from President Georges Pompidou in 1971. When news of the pardon became public, a national scandal ensued, and Touvier once again went into hiding. He was arrested finally in 1989 by French police at a monastery in Nice. In March–April 1994, Touvier was tried and convicted of crimes against humanity for ordering the June 29, 1944, execution of seven Jews at the cemetery of Ril-

of justice in the case of René Bousquet, the former Vichy chief of police.[3] (Whether these trials were themselves justified is another question.) The second attitude, that of virtuous indignation, characterizes various committees of "vigilance" or those who fight out of "duty to memory," all of whom like to point an accusing finger at the real or supposed weaknesses of others. In both cases, and in spite of opposition between their value judgments, the people holding these attitudes raise arguments in contiguity with the past rather than introducing a comparative perspective into the discussion; they hold strictly to the events themselves without seeking to extract their exemplary meaning.

My interest in the episode in wartime Saint-Amand derives from two sources: a fortuitous one (which I explain in the preface to the original edition of this book) and another, more general one that I would like to mention here. My own past in a totalitarian country (I grew up and studied in Bulgaria until the age of twenty-four) has made me immune to the temptations of moral relativism. I know that political evil exists and that it is not to be confused with the insufficiencies of the political system in which I live today in France. I also know that this evil is absolutely frightening. But at the same time, it is not as foreign to us as we, the free subjects of a liberal democracy, would like it to be; in general, there is nothing monstrous or savage about the actors in this evil. It therefore seems to me that a comforting Manichaeism is every bit as harmful as moral relativism. I also believe that one must struggle

---

lieux-la-Pape in reprisal for the Resistance's murder of Vichy's minister of information, Philippe Henriot, the day before. For details of Touvier's life and trial, see Richard J. Golsan, ed., *Memory, the Holocaust, and French Justice: The Bousquet and Touvier Affairs* (Hanover, N.H.: University Press of New England, 1996).

3. René Bousquet, named head of Vichy police in 1942 by Pierre Laval, was charged with working with Nazi authorities to organize the roundup and deportation of French and foreign Jews throughout France in 1942–1943. The best-known roundup occurred in July 1942, when some thirteen thousand foreigners were gathered up by French police and herded into the bicycle racing stadium known as the Vélodrome d'Hiver (or Vél d'Hiv), kept there in abominable conditions for several days, and later deported to the east. After the war, Bousquet became a successful banker and businessman, whose many influential friends included François Mitterrand. In the late 1980s Bousquet was charged with crimes against humanity but was gunned down by a crazed publicity seeker in the summer of 1993 before he could stand trial. For Bousquet's career, see Golsan, *Memory*.

against the willingness to renounce values and to surrender the aspiration to greater justice just as, at the same time, one must avoid the easy habit of identifying oneself with good heroes or good victims by depicting the wicked as totally different from oneself.

For this reason it is imperative that one look closely at the past, with its violent moments that act as a magnifying glass and allow for a clearer observation of the most somber sides of human conduct. I therefore read this story of militiamen and resisters, a story of the past, without abandoning the ethical categories that are mine in the present—not to condemn, or praise, or absolve the characters of the past (they are almost all dead today, and it is not my intention to teach lessons to the survivors of yesteryear) but to try to understand better wherein lies danger and wherein lies hope. We cannot intervene in the past and undo the events that took place, but we can at least try to understand them so that nonsense is not added to horror.

Acknowledgments

I wish to express my sincere thanks, first of all, to everyone who was kind enough to share with me their memories of the period. Next, to the people who gave me helpful advice and provided me with needed documents, in particular Madame Chantal Bonazzi at the National Archives and Monsieur Jean-Yves Ribault at the Departmental Archives of the Cher, as well as Jean-Pierre Azéma, Maxime Chagnon, Jacques Delperrié de Bayac, and Alain Rafesthain.

Finally, to Annick Jacquet, with whom I conducted the interviews, who transcribed them, and whose suggestions have been useful to me at every stage of this work; and to Nancy Huston, who collaborated with me on writing a first draft of the story of these events.

T.T.

TRANSLATOR'S NOTE

Tzvetan Todorov's references to works listed in the bibliography following the text appear parenthetically within the text, as they did in the original edition of A *French Tragedy*. Footnotes intended for American readers have been added to the present edition by Richard J. Golsan and Tzvetan Todorov.

I would like to thank Richard J. Golsan for his kindness and the valuable suggestions he gave me throughout my work on this translation. I thank as well my husband, Van Kelly, and Hélène Germain-Simoes, both of whom offered me encouragement and helpful advice.

My work on this book is dedicated to the memory of Annie Katz, a special friend who first introduced me to earlier works by Tzvetan Todorov. I will always be grateful that at a critical stage in my education, she so generously shared with me her language, her culture, and her home.

M.B.K.

PROLOGUE

As I began reading the newspaper that morning, I was surprised to come across the name of the town of Saint-Amand-Montrond. It was there because of a matter long since past, a particularly revolting massacre dating back to the days of the Occupation. There were two distinct reasons for my surprise. The first and totally fortuitous one was that at that very moment my newspaper and I happened to be in the Saint-Amand area, where I was settled for the year. The second, less anecdotal reason was that no one ever speaks of Saint-Amand in the "national" press. God knows this town prides itself on being situated in the geographical center of France (actually, several neighboring villages make the same claim), but that is not enough to attract lasting media attention. Like so many other medium-size towns cast with a pervasive gloominess, this town seems remarkable only for its lack of any significant events; it is truly a quiet little spot where, as they say, nothing happens. Is this really the place where fifty years ago a particularly memorable event took place? An event I'd never heard of in the more than twenty years that I'd been coming to this region? There was plenty here to stir my curiosity.

I asked around; nobody knew much about it. I went to the town library; they said they had only vaguely heard of it, nothing more. A group of Jews had been rounded up in Saint-Amand during the summer of 1944 and killed in the wells of Guerry, not far away. I was nevertheless able to obtain a few references: a "real-life" account published at the time, a commemorative brochure, and the work of a historian of the local Resistance. These texts contained many names unknown to me, and I wanted to learn more about them; other books came to my attention. Little by little I realized that the massacre in question had not occurred at that time and place for no reason but was rather the culmination of a series of no less dramatic events that preceded it during that summer. After a short time I was no longer satisfied with having read the few works that told the various episodes in this story. With the help of a friend from the region, I decided to seek out and ask questions of the various contemporaries and witnesses of these incidents. I ran across some unpublished manuscripts. I read both the daily and weekly press of the period, and I spend several days undoing the strings around dusty files in the departmental and national archives. I could no longer tear myself away from the story.

It is true that this story seems to illustrate particularly well a page from the recent history of France—the Liberation of 1944—as it was lived out far from the front lines. Here, strangely enough, the war of the French against the Germans recedes into the background, and the ruthless civil war waged by militiamen and Resistance fighters, French against French, takes center stage.

The Germans are not totally absent from this story, but they assume minor roles. For one thing, their institutions embodied the Fascist ideology from which the militia drew inspiration (without Germany, the militia would never have existed); they also established an interpretation of anti-Semitism, embodied by the Gestapo, that went so far as to include the physical destruction of the Jews. Furthermore, the German army provided brute force, which was essential to carrying out plans instigated elsewhere. But for the most part, it is French people who must be held responsible for what happened.

The story of the Liberation in Saint-Amand also reveals the complex implications of the Allied landing, the sometimes unrewarding role reserved for the Resistance, and the strained relations between interior resistance and exterior forces, between members

of the Resistance and the civilian population, and further, between Communist and non-Communist members of the Resistance or (and this is not always the same thing) between extreme
radicals and moderates. With the executions that mark the final
phase, it illustrates as well the potential for tragic endings: mas-
sacres that are shocking even if they are not the worst that would
be experienced during the summer of 1944.

Finally, this story prompts an ethical debate, for unlike certain
other episodes in the Liberation or the Occupation, it not only
shows the confrontation of abstract entities—the "Germans," the
"collaborators," the "Resistance members," the "civilian population"—but also brings individuals to grips with one another and
thus puts into play their personal responsibility. In reading about
their fate I became convinced that, when talking about this period, it was imperative to get beyond both the hagiography of the
"victors" (which is nevertheless so fitting for official celebrations)
and its reverse image, systematic denigration; the same could be
said for the "defeated." Instead of a world of black and white, I discovered a series of distinct situations, of particular acts, each of
which called for its own separate evaluation.

But that was not all there was in the story of Saint-Amand that
so interested me. After all, provided you dig deep enough, almost
any story can take on this sort of exemplary force. For me at least,
something else made the events of Saint-Amand particularly com-
pelling. I could not shake the feeling that someone had conceived
and articulated all these actions in the same way that a writer of
tragedy would. I am not a believer, I have not been in communication with Providence nor with the Creator, and yet everything
was happening here as if One had wanted to produce an aesthet-
ically perfect form. Without question, this form was that of a
tragedy, despite several interludes during which tensions were
temporarily eased or there was even comic relief. It was a tragedy
both because, once in motion, everything seemed to be intercon-
nected with an implacable rigor and because the causes of calami-

ty were not contingent and could not be pushed aside—evil ensued from goodness itself; it seemed unavoidable.

I hesitated a long time over what form to give to this exemplary story. Not being Shakespeare, I immediately rejected the most suitable one, that of a proper tragedy. And yet the mere publication of a few eyewitness reports would not have been enough to bring to light all the essential aspects of the story. I therefore opted for a hybrid solution. One the one hand, and with the approval of his descendants, I published (in the French edition of this book) the memoirs of the mayor of that time, René Sadrin, concerning these events. A key witness as well as a player in certain episodes, the mayor compiled his memories in the aftermath of the war, then reworked them in 1956. On the other hand, I wrote a reconstitution of the events as they appeared to me at the end of my research; it is therefore based on the published or unpublished recollections of various witnesses, the list of whom can be found at the end of my account.

I have done all I possibly could to establish the truth of the facts, but precisely because I spent a lot of time looking for it, I know that the truth remains a fragile thing; tomorrow I could discover some details, some implications of the acts that I describe, that have eluded me and that would change the overall meaning. Everything that follows must therefore be read in light of this explicit limitation: "according to what I know at present."

THE CHARACTERS

Members of the Resistance

René Van Gaver, age 37, leader of the Combat movement in Saint-Amand

Daniel Blanchard, age 25, military head of the Combat movement

Georges Chaillaud, age 28, one of Van Gaver's lieutenants

Georges Le Quellec, age 30, another of Van Gaver's lieutenants

André Sagnelonge, age 37, brother-in-law of Blanchard

Hubert Lalonnier, age 37, leader of the FTP (*Franc-Tireurs* and Partisans)

Fernand Sochet, age 29, leader of the National Front[4]

Commander "François" (pseudonym in the Resistance), age 37, leader of the FFI (French Forces of the Interior) of the Creuse region

Lieutenant "Roger" (pseudonym in the Resistance), age 29, under the orders of Commander "François"

Colonel Bertrand, age 49, leader of the FFI of the Cher-Sud region

The Traitor, age and profession unspecified

Militiamen and Collaborators

Francis Bout de l'An, age 34, secretary-general of the militia

Simone Bout de l'An, age 34, his wife

4. The National Front was a patriotic organization created by the French Communist Party which functioned during the Occupation and into the postwar years. It should not be confused with Jean Marie Le Pen's extreme right wing National Front, active in French politics today.

Auguste Vigier, age 33, regional head of the militia
Joseph Lécussan, age 49, militia officer, then subprefect of Saint-Amand[5]
Clément Marchand, age 28, militiaman, *chef de trentaine*[6]
Louis Bastide, age 34, militiaman, *chef de trentaine*
André Rochelet, age 30, lieutenant under Lécussan
Roger Thévenot, age 41, leader of the militia in Bourges
Pierre-Marie Paoli, age 23, works at the Gestapo in Bourges

The Civilian Population

René Sadrin, age 63, mayor of Saint-Amand
François Villatte, age 31, bureau chief at the subprefecture
Bernard Delalande, age 39, employee at the subprefecture
Msgr. Joseph Lefebvre, archbishop of Bourges
Théogène Chavaillon, age 44, pharmacist
Thérèse Lamoureux, age 16, young girl of Orval, a suburb of Saint-Amand
Chaskel (Charles) Krameisen, age 44, Jewish refugee
Marthe Krameisen, age 51, Jewish refugee, his wife
Camille Guillemin, age 44, farmer

Other episodic characters

Time: summer 1944. Place: the center of France.

---

5. France is divided into departments, each under the authority of a prefect, a functionary appointed by the national government. The geographical unit, the department, thus coincides with the administrative unit, known as the prefecture. Each prefecture is subdivided into subprefectures under the direction of subprefects. The prefecture of the Cher department is located in the city of Bourges. Saint-Amand is the administrative seat of one of the southern subprefectures of the Cher department.

6. According to Jacques Delperrié de Bayac, the *trentaine*, a unit consisting of thirty men, was the third smallest unit in the military organization of the militia. Smaller units included the *dizaine* (ten men) and the *main* (five men). Larger units included the *centaine* (one hundred men, consisting of three *trentaines* and a *dizaine* of officers) and a *cohorte*, made up of three *centaines* and a command group. The largest organizational unit, the *centre*, was composed of three or four *cohortes*. See *Histoire de la milice*, 1918–1945 (Paris: Fayard, 1969), 182.

A FRENCH TRAGEDY

THE UPRISING

The Decision

At six o'clock in the morning of June 6, 1944, a meeting takes place in the home of René Van Gaver in Coust, about ten kilometers southeast of Saint-Amand. The participants were summoned during the night. In addition to Van Gaver, the chief of the Combat resistance movement for the Cher-Sud region, those attending are Daniel Blanchard, Van Gaver's assistant in charge of military affairs (known as Surcouf); Hubert Lalonnier, the head of the FTP (or FFTP), (French) *Franc-tireurs* and Partisans (the Communist maquis) for the region; and another member of the FTP, an official of the Communist Party in the Cher region. Van Gaver has called these local Resistance leaders together to inform them that the landing of the Allies is under way and to decide what time the takeover of Saint-Amand will begin. This is in fact the day that a tremendous action must be carried out: the town, which has been occupied for four years, will be liberated! The operations are set to begin at 6:00 P.M., and all are to meet at the lock at Clairins, halfway to Saint-Amand. Various technical details are finalized.

The decision itself to take over the town on the day of the landing was actually made sometime earlier. But when, exactly? In all likelihood, on May 31, 1944. On that day in the very town of Saint-Amand, perhaps in a back room of the café La Chaumière, also owned by Van Gaver, another important meeting took place. During this meeting the two largest Resistance organizations in the region, Combat and the FTP, decided to coordinate their action and to work under a single command. Present at this first meeting were Van Gaver and Blanchard for Combat and Lalonnier and Henry Diaz for the FTP. The encounter was organized and conducted by the departmental (that is to say, regional) official of the National Front, Fernand Sochet.

At this point it is necessary to digress a bit in order to understand the makeup of the Resistance of 1944, a veritable maquis, made even more impenetrable by the craze for acronyms and abbreviations characteristic of the time. To put it in simple terms, there are first of all two great families, the Communists and the non-Communists, the latter especially dispersed. For example, since 1942, Blanchard, like many others in the military, has belonged to the Alliance network, which works for the British intelligence. Van Gaver is the local official of Combat, a movement that itself resulted from the fusion of several groups. Through the impetus given by Jean Moulin,[7] these movements had begun to regroup themselves; in January 1943, Combat, Libération, and Franc-Tireur united in the MUR (United Movements for Resistance), which in December 1943 became the MLN (Movement for National Liberation). The Secret Army (AS) was for a while the armed branch of these organizations. It can thus be said that Van Gaver and Blanchard are members of Combat as much as they are of the MUR or the MLN or even of the AS.

On the Communist side, things are a lot simpler. There is but one organization, the FTP. But as usual, the Party has also created a supposedly independent "mass" organization that really is entirely under its command. This is the FN (National Front), an avatar of the Popular Front but with a patriotic reorientation that suits the era; on the surface, its political program boils down to "kicking the Krauts out of France," which gives it wide appeal.

7. Jean Moulin (1899–1943) was a high functionary in the French Resistance. Assigned (by de Gaulle) the mission of unifying the Resistance, Moulin was parachuted into France in 1942. After being named president of the National Council of the Resistance in 1943, he was arrested by the Gestapo and executed shortly thereafter.

In 1944 the convergence begun in 1943 of all these Resistance groups comes to pass. The coordination of the FTP, the MUR, and the ORA (Resistance Organization of the Army, made up of former military members) gives rise to the FFI (French Forces of the Interior), created in December 1943 and directed by the CNR (National Council for the Resistance), whose military arm will be the COMAC (Military Action Committee). The Communists succeed in gaining command of these national authorities.

At the time of the June 6 meeting, the COMAC is directed by three members, two of whom, Maurice Kriegel-Valrimont and Pierre Villon, are affiliated with the Party. Alfred Malleret-Joinville, COMAC chief of staff, likewise follows its directives. One of the initial leaders of Combat is in Algiers, the other is in prison: thus, Marcel Dégliame-Fouché, a Communist sympathizer, becomes the movement's representative to the CNR and leader of the COMAC for the Southern Zone.[8] As a result of this evolution in the leadership of the Resistance, the non-Communist voice would no longer be heard were it not for the representatives of Free France outside the country. It is the Resistance on one side and London and Algiers (de Gaulle and his representatives) on the other: General Koenig, in theory the head of all French forces; Jacques Chaban-Delmas,[9] delegated to the COMAC by de Gaulle,

8. After the armistice of June 1940, France was divided into two zones. The Northern, or Occupied, Zone included Paris and was occupied by the German army. The Southern Zone, also known as the Free Zone, was governed by the French from the resort town of Vichy and maintained a measure of autonomy during the first few years of the Occupation. In November 1942 the German army occupied the Southern Zone as well, but Vichy's administrative role was not affected. The demarcation line between the two zones passed through the middle of the Cher Department, separating the prefecture at Bourges, in the Occupied Zone, from the subprefecture at Saint-Amand, in the Free Zone. The Resistance observed the same divisions. Resistance headquarters for the southern Cher, in the Free Zone, was independent of its analogue in the northern Cher, in the Occupied Zone.

9. A major figure in the Resistance from the early years of the Occupation, Jacques Chaban-Delmas had a distinguished political career in the postwar years. Elected deputy from the Gironde region in 1946 and mayor of Bordeaux in 1947, he served in various ministerial posts during the Fourth Republic and, an avowed Gaullist, served as Georges Pompidou's prime minister from 1969 to 1972. Chaban-Delmas was an unsuccessful candidate for the presidency in 1974. For Chaban-Delmas's resistance activities and postwar career, see Olivier Wieviorka, *Nous entrerons dans la carrière: De la Résistance à l'exercice du pouvoir* (Paris: Seuil, 1994), 291–323.

and the military delegates of each region (the center of France falls within the R5 [Region 5], whose capital is Limoges).

In sum, the military leadership of the Resistance in May 1944 is in the hands of the Communists. Add to this the fact that this leadership has adopted an extremist position: it is calling for a national insurrection to go along with the landing of the Allies; furthermore, it wants to maintain a certain autonomy vis-à-vis London and Algiers and reserves the right to take its own initiatives. As the days pass, its position becomes more extreme. COMAC directive No. 10, issued on May 29, 1944, is particularly explicit:

In the weeks to come, every man must prove that he is worthy of his post: (a) by the loyal application of COMAC decisions . . . . : immediate action, distribution of arms, implementation of plans . . . ; (b) by the manner in which, in the struggle against the enemy, in the operations to be executed in conjunction with the landing and the allied offensive, and in the insurrectional battles of our people, he is able to show initiative, daring, clairvoyance, and the spirit of sacrifice and devotion to the nation. (Kriegel-Valrimont, 31)

Therein lies the basic program of action: arms distribution and the implementation of "plans" (the Green Plan: destruction of railroad lines; the Tortoise Plan: the blocking of roads; etc.) but also a call to go beyond the basic program, an open door to an increasing buildup in the manifestations of the fighting spirit. But even if the "spirit of sacrifice" can ultimately be summoned, it is a wholly different story for "clairvoyance."

The prevailing attitude of the leadership of the Resistance is even more clearly revealed in the documents written at the time of the landing. On June 6, D-day itself, the high command of the FTP Southern Zone circulates an "Order of the Day." This document, after calling for national insurrection (to ensure the presence of French forces along with those of the Allies and to play on patriotic feelings), the massive recruitment of men, and the distribution of arms, recommends: "Wherever the relationship of forces permits—such is the case as of today in the immense provinces of Savoie, the Alps, the Massif central and the Limousin—get everything under way for the liberation of these territories in order to turn them into bases of resistance and attack" (Guingouin, 178). On June 14, in response to a directive from Koenig, which will be discussed later, Kriegel-Valrimont, in the name of the COMAC, writes: "National insurrection . . . is a vital necessity for our country. . . . Insurrection is more economical than waiting for liberation by the Allies. Only national insurrection, liberation gained through the sacrifices of the nation itself . . . will give our country a new soul" (Kriegel-Valrimont, 41–42).

In issuing these directives, the military command of the Resistance carries out the decisions made by the political leadership of the PCF (French Communist Party). In fact, it is no longer composed of militants directly engaged in the action; an effective roundup by the Gestapo cut off the head of the leadership of the FTP for the Southern Zone in the spring of 1944. As Georges Guingouin, head of the Limousin maquis recalls, "[now] it is the underground secretariat of the Communist Party, including Léon Mauvais, Raymond Guyot and Eugène Hénaff, that will give out its instructions as long as its leadership is not reconstituted. But these 'politicians' fail to take into account the military realities. Setting off the insurrection is one thing, but taking over open towns and, above all, holding them are quite another!" (Guingouin, 175). In fact, it is undeniable that advocating insurrection and the liberation of territory (for example, in the Limousin region, to which the Cher-Sud area is connected) on the day of the Allied landing is an act of suicide. The superiority of the opposing forces is such that it leaves no doubt as to the outcome of the conflict: on one side, standing troops, heavily armed and well trained for combat; on the other side, crowds of enthusiastic but inexperienced young men armed with a few makeshift weapons. Indeed, the course of operations over the summer of 1944 demonstrates the real relationship of forces; the liberation of France will not take three days, as the leaders of the Resistance seem to think, but rather three months.

What explains this suicidal attitude, which the Resistance leaders had to recognize as such, judging from the frequent recurrence of their calls for the necessary sacrifice? Enthralled as they might be by their own speeches, the leaders of the Party do not seriously think the Resistance fighters are capable of taking on the standing German forces. But they prefer death in combat to waiting prudently—it is a more "economical" solution, to quote Kriegel-Valrimont's brutal expression—especially when the ones making the decision are not the same ones who will die. The Party is not seeking to take power directly, as it was sometimes accused of doing. Although the local leaders do not lack the desire to do so, such are not the directives from Moscow to which they are subject. But the Party does wish to improve substantially its position on the postwar French political chessboard; to become, if possible, the foremost party in France and to shift the future evolution of the country in its favor. To do this, it plans to take every possible advantage of the "capital" accumulated by the Resistance. The "party of the executed"[10] already enjoys an incontestable moral prestige. The sacrifice of the militants and the sympathizers, far from damaging the Party's reputation, will enhance it powerfully. By engaging in the insurrection on June 6, the Party cannot lose: either it succeeds directly and attains power or it fails, but its partners then contract a debt that they will someday have to repay. This line of reasoning should not be interpreted as evidence of excessive Machiavellianism; the Communist leaders are sincerely convinced that resurrection demands preconditional sacrifice and that such sacrifice is the only means of acquiring a "new soul."

10. In the years following World War II, the French Communist Party liked to call itself the "Party of 75,000 Executed" in reference to the number of its members shot by the Germans during the Occupation. Such sacrifices, the Party hoped, would benefit it politically in the postwar struggles for power. A fuller discussion of the Communist memory of the war can be found in Henry Rousso, *The Vichy Syndrome: History and Memory in France since 1944* (Cambridge, Mass.: Harvard University Press, 1991).

Having received the instructions from Limoges of May 29, 1944, Fernand Sochet calls a meeting of the various Resistance organizations. In truth, this meeting does not include everyone and is rather odd. Several days earlier, on May 20, the different Resistance movements of Saint-Amand had already unified within the FFI and entrusted their leadership to Colonel Bertrand. Bertrand's views are in keeping with those of the ORA, and he is loyal to the exterior command (to de Gaulle). He belonged to the First RI (Infantry Regiment), which settled in Saint-Amand just after the defeat and has preserved its fighting spirit. This unit was disarmed and dissolved in November 1942, immediately following the occupation of the Free Zone, and was replaced by the First RF (Regiment of France), an armed force in the service of the Vichy regime. After some hesitancy and several attempts at rapprochement with the Pétain supporters, Bertrand joined the Resistance, and since 1943 he has been the local chief of the ORA. Based on his military experience, the COMAC chooses him to lead the FFI of the Morvan region, to which the southern part of the Cher region is now attached. However, not only has Bertrand not called the meeting to prepare the insurrection, he is not even invited to the one organized by Sochet! Among the Communists he has the reputation of being overly cautious and of holding an *attentiste*[11] attitude. A former Communist Resistance member, describing his relations with Bertrand, told us in 1993, "It was as if we had a souped-up race car and he had nothing but a bicycle."

Sochet brings together the two other branches of the Resistance: the FTP and the MUR, or in this case, Combat. The role of unifier that he assigns himself is characteristic. Fernand Sochet is a militant Communist. As a prisoner of war he escaped and returned to the Cher region in June 1943, where he resumed working as a teacher in Vierzon, a nearby city, and found himself in

11. The term *attentiste* was a generally pejorative term applied to those who hesitated to take sides during the Occupation, preferring instead to "wait and see" who the victors would turn out to be.

charge of the FTP intelligence. Upon noticing that he might be suspected of engaging in illegal activity, he asked for and received a medical leave, which permitted him to devote himself full-time to the Resistance and to live from then on in semihiding. In January 1944, however, he left his job at the FTP to become the departmental organizer of the National Front, an organization that was in principle independent of the Party and claimed to arise from pure patriotic spirit. This "neutral" unifier called together representatives of the two Resistance groups (other than the ORA): Lalonnier and Diaz for the FTP, Van Gaver and Blanchard for Combat.

The paths that lead these four individuals to the meeting of May 31 are very different. Hubert Lalonnier and Henry Diaz are veterans of the International Brigades of Spain; they are relatively experienced fighters. They had not met in 1936, however. They met in 1943 at Dun-sur-Auron, a small town in the Cher where Diaz, a prisoner of war, was taking refuge after his escape. They managed to procure weapons by recovering, among others, the ones that the veterans of the First RI had hidden; in all, they have retrieved fourteen machine guns and thirty-two carbine rifles. With the number of those who refuse to work in the STO (Forced Work Service in Germany)[12] increasing as of 1943, Lalonnier and Diaz have been scouring the villages to recruit them, provide food to them if they are hiding in the forest, and also to teach them how to handle weapons. Their group already has undertaken a bold raid, the rescue of a wounded comrade at the hospital of Saint-Amand. But this same action also reveals the lack of rigor in their organization; the one comrade was freed, it is true, but they accidentally killed another, whose body they left behind in front of the

12. The Service du Travail Obligatoire (STO), implemented by Pierre Laval in February 1943 under pressure from the Germans, was a conscription program that sent young Frenchmen to Germany to work in factories to help the Nazi war effort. The program was tremendously unpopular. Many Frenchmen, faced with the choice of working in German factories under threat of Allied bombardment or joining the Resistance, chose the latter option. The STO and its causes and effects are discussed in Robert Paxton, *Vichy France: Old Guard and New Order, 1940–1944* (New York: Columbia University Press, 1972).

hospital. A former blue-collar worker from Bordeaux who plays a major role in the FTP, Lalonnier has the reputation of being a tough guy, a risk-taker who nevertheless knows how to protect his men when need be. He is handsome, enterprising, and articulate.

René Van Gaver is a native of the Jura, where he worked as a bureaucrat before the war. He was the director of the Office départemental de placement de la main-d'oeuvre (departmental employment office) and also regional secretary for the Radical and Radical-Socialist Federation.[13] Known for his anti-Pétain views, he was dismissed from his job. He then came with his wife and two children to Saint-Amand, a very quiet place in the Free Zone. Being a man with some financial means at his disposal, Van Gaver bought the Rex movie theater downtown, a home in town, and a villa in Coust. He is an urbanite, a government worker, a man who is used to political talk. An innocuous man gazing myopically from behind his big tortoiseshell glasses, the owner-operator of the movie theater is known for his punctiliousness and affability. In reality, in 1943 he joined the Combat network that was created in the region in late 1942 and soon afterward became its leader, replacing the printer Bussière. Combat's social recruitment clearly differs from that of the FTP—rather than workers or poor farmers, its recruits are property owners, self-employed craftsmen, and clerks.

Daniel Blanchard was born in Garches, in the region of Paris. He studied for admission into the Ecole normale d'instituteurs (teachers college) and worked at the mayor's office. Mobilized at the beginning of the war in the First RI, he attained the rank of officer cadet. After the regiment was disbanded in November 1942, he remained in Saint-Amand, where he married and found a job

13. Members of the Radical-Socialist Party, known as Radicals, were moderate left republicans whose hearts were on the left but whose pocketbooks were on the right, according to Eugen Weber. The Radicals joined forces with the Socialists and Communists in the mid-1930s to create the Popular Front, the last left-wing government in France before the Occupation. Party leaders included Camille Chautemps, Edouard Herriot, and Edouard Daladier, men whose reputations were later sullied by political scandal and poor political judgment. Daladier, for instance, was France's leader during the Munich crisis.

in the insurance field. He is a young man who impresses his friends with his speaking ability, his physical grace, and his character; he is a good and noble individual. In 1942, Van Gaver bought the café La Chaumière owned by Blanchard's future mother-in-law, and the two men became friends. Recruited from the Alliance, Blanchard became the military head of Combat; he had more experience in the matter than Van Gaver. The clandestine activities of Combat, whose members numbered about thirty in 1943, essentially boil down to creating and maintaining the network itself, listening to Radio London, and handing out leaflets. Efforts are also made to protect other members of the underground or those evading the STO by providing them with hiding places and food ration cards. Combat possesses some arms received in the recent parachute drops from London, but it has not yet undertaken any military actions. During May 1944, Van Gaver and Blanchard are not thinking in terms of political strategy; they are honestly dreaming of the liberation of their homeland.

What was said at the clandestine meeting of May 31? We do not know exactly. But we do know what came out of it: first, an assignment of roles that, strangely enough, fails to take into account Colonel Bertrand, the theoretical head of the Resistance. The other movements (without the ORA), gathered together, appoint an administrative head (Van Gaver, assisted by the "federative" Sochet) and a military leader (Lalonnier, with Blanchard as second in command). Most important, a vital decision is made: on the day of the Allied landing the Resistance fighters will occupy the town of Saint-Amand. If all goes well, they will thereby be participating in the "liberation of the territory"; if not, they will take the opportunity to recruit and arm scores of new Resistance members. They will then pull back into the more densely wooded Creuse region nearby. There they would be within the foothills of the Massif central, an isolated and rugged region more difficult to access than the area of Saint-Amand, which, although lush with several big forests, is a region of farmlands crossed by major roads.

But this second alternative is not taken very seriously; optimism is the order of the day.

Sochet presented the directives of the COMAC as orders of insurrection. Even today veteran Resistance members maintain that Saint-Amand was taken over "on orders from Limoges," if not from London. But can one really talk about "orders" in this circumstance? The Resistance does not follow military discipline, far from it; moreover, if it did, it would have to be under Bertrand. It is a question of recommendations rather than of orders in the strict sense of the word; local leaders have their say. The proof is the diversity of reactions to the directive sent out by the R5, a diversity that corresponds not to the FTP–MLN split but rather to the extent of the leader's military experience. Thus, the head of the FFI of the Creuse region, the very anti-FTP Commander "François," opts for the insurrection and occupation of Guéret, as do certain FTP leaders of the Corrèze region, thereby bringing about the dramatic events of Tulle: occupation of the town by Resistance members, death by execution of the German garrison, and reprisals made by an SS attack force, resulting in 99 hanged and 101 dead in deportation. For his part, the FTP member Georges Guingouin, who dominates the Resistance of the Limousin region, reacts totally differently, as he himself recalls: "Molinier . . . transmits the order to take Limoges. An order so absurd that . . . Bricout calls a meeting of those in charge. . . . All these comrades [except one] come down on Bricout's side. . . . Guingouin, contacted, refuses" (Guingouin, 175). The rest is history: the town of Limoges will surrender to Guingouin, without bloodshed, but only on August 21, two and a half months after the landing.

Van Gaver and Blanchard, however, do not have the authority of Guingouin, who has been fighting in the maquis since 1940 and whose prestige in the region is immense. And besides, it is not at all certain that they would have sought to oppose the directives from Limoges, even though former Resistance members cite tactical differences between the two and give the impression that the leaders of Combat let Sochet and Lalonnier force their hand somewhat. The meetings of the Resistance take place in a specifically masculine atmosphere (wives are kept totally ignorant of the preparations), and one thing is certain: it is more manly to fight than to wait. There is a climate of overstatement: precisely because they have not yet proved themselves the way Lalonnier and Diaz have, Van Gaver and Blanchard cannot allow themselves to lag behind. They must, if possible, appear even more determined than their comrades, more courageous, more imbued with the spirit of sacrifice mentioned in the directives.

But we must not go looking for faulty motives only in Van Gaver's and Blanchard's acquiescence. After all, they both have a certain political experience, they have been taking risks for some time now, and they can be held responsible for their actions rather than viewed as puppets manipulated by the Communists or by circumstances, even if this manipulation undeniably took place. Van Gaver and Blanchard want France to rise up and fight because they think it humiliating to wait for others to bring about liberation. To their minds, national dignity asserts itself through action taken on one's own. Thus, the French must hurry to liberate their homeland themselves instead of letting other people do it for them. They are risking their lives, and they know it, but what good is a life without dignity? It is with the best intentions that the Resistance leaders make their decision on May 31; and that is why, instead of being merely wrong, the decision is tragic.

Having emerged from their discussions, Van Gaver and Blanchard nevertheless feel obligated to inform Colonel Bertrand of the results (it is significant that the FTP, supposedly an integral part of the FFI, does not handle this). Blanchard, from having served in the First RI, knows the colonel well; they are to meet on June 2. Bertrand explained several times, after the war, how the meeting unfolded (he speaks of himself in the third person). Van Gaver and Blanchard tell him they have received the orders from "their leaders in Limoges" and, to spare his feelings, claim not to be in contact with the FTP. They invite him to join in the takeover of Saint-Amand the day of the landing and to destroy the forces of the militia that they find there; failing that, he is asked to prevent the First RF, stationed in Saint-Amand and the surrounding area and the only major military force in the region, from intervening against them when the insurrection takes place.

On the first point, Bertrand is in total disagreement and informs Van Gaver and Blanchard of "the unconditional orders to wait that he had received for the first period of the landing" (*Le Berry républicain*, September 16, 1964). This *attentisme* of Bertrand does, in fact, strictly correspond to the political line decided on by de Gaulle. Secret instructions dated May 16, 1944, and signed by de Gaulle specify that "at the time of the initial landings, a rash, general engagement of the totality of the various units of the Army of the Interior that are still in the formative stage is likely to sap all the energy of the French Resistance and substantially harm, without recompense, the fate of all French people" (Azéma and Bédarida, 2:396). But although theoretically the head of the FFI of the Cher, Bertrand has little authority over his subordinates; thus, they have to admit openly the failure of negotiations. On the second point he appears more cooperative. He alerts some friends within the First RF on the next day, June 3, so that they will speak with his boss in Saint-Amand, Commander Ardisson, on behalf of Van Gaver and Blanchard (cf. *Les Bandes de Picardie*, 65–66).

Does he tell himself, as Van Gaver and Blanchard take leave of him, that these young men are getting themselves involved in a suicidal adventure and that this is probably the last time he will ever see them? The fact remains that on June 5 he leaves Saint-Amand for the Morvan region to assume direction of his unit on June 6, and he will not return to the Cher until July 20. At this point, Bertrand disappears from our story.

Do Van Gaver and Blanchard have doubts after this lukewarm reception and the promise to help only indirectly? Some of their comrades, informed of the decision, find it premature. However, the day's events make them think that there is some urgency to take action. On the same day, June 2, after their visit at Bertrand's, they learn that the Gestapo has arrested a high-ranking person, Sub-prefect Lecène, and accused him of being an important leader of the Resistance. Van Gaver and Blanchard did not know that he was (Lecène belonged to the very same Combat movement but at a different level; the local heads were not kept informed), but that does not keep them from taking the information seriously—it means the Resistance is in danger. On Sunday, June 4, Blanchard, accompanied by his brother-in-law André Sagnelonge, also in the Resistance, takes part in a small party in the next town, Château-meillant. The two men have a lot to drink. His wife reproaches him for it, and Blanchard turns to her and says, "You know, this is our last chance to get drunk." The sacrifice is assumed, from that time on.

The next day, June 5, they are glued to the radio, but the infor-mation they receive is ambiguous. On the one hand, they feel they have made the right decision. Indeed, on this day London broad-casts all of the "personal messages," that is to say, it puts the French Resistance as a whole on alert. The decision to do so was made by the military command of the Allied forces (by Eisenhower) with the aim of throwing German intelligence off the track—it is not any one region that is concerned with the landing; it is all of them! Isn't the very overabundance of messages a sign to rise up? But on the other hand, if they follow to the letter the message transmitted specifically to them, they can draw no such conclusion. "In the Norman plain there is a big book" means for them: state of alert, implementation of the "plans" (destruction of railway lines, tele-phone lines, etc.) but not insurrection. The state of their confu-sion is clearly reflected in a speech by one of the surviving leaders of the insurrection, Georges Chaillaud, on June 6, 1946, as he seeks to explain the decision to occupy the town. What he says they were supposed to do was implement the Iron Plan—"sabo-tage of communication lines, actions to knock out the traitors' ability to do harm, guerrilla actions against the occupation troops sent as reinforcement on the operations front." He concludes, "We executed this plan at the specified time" (*La Voix républicaine*, June 15, 1946), not noticing that the action of insurrection and occupation of the town does not figure in his own enumeration.

But June 5, 1944, is no time to waver. The dice have been thrown; there is no going back. On the evening of that day, Van Gaver receives the announcement of the now imminent landing, and he therefore convenes the leaders of the Resistance for the morning of June 6. When the discussion is over, the leaders go off to their assigned tasks. They will get together again in twelve hours.

A Quiet Day

On the morning of June 6, Simone Bout de l'An is at 7 rue du Commandant-Martin, a beautiful private mansion located in the center of Saint-Amand and occupied since April 1944 by the forces of the militia. This political, military police, an outgrowth of the Service d'ordre légionnaire (the Légion was the veteran's organization under Pétain) directed by Joseph Darnand, was officially created on January 30, 1943; on February 28 of the same year a local chapter was organized at Saint-Amand. It has been fairly successful: in December 1943 militia members there numbered 205, of whom 105 were *francs-gardes* (armed fighters); beyond the central core there were the *trentaines* in the small neighboring towns of Lignières, Culan, and Sancoins.

In April 1944 the assistant secretary-general of the militia, Francis Bout de l'An, traveled to Saint-Amand for a political meeting, and during his stay there he had an idea. For some time he had been looking for a quiet spot where he could leave his family: his wife, Simone; his two sons; and his mother. He himself lived in Vichy most of the time, but he considered it a little too dangerous;

besides, he liked to keep a little distance away from his family
obligations. Saint-Amand seemed to be the ideal spot: a town of
about ten thousand inhabitants, a subprefecture in the southern
part of the department (or region) of the Cher, in the center of a
relatively prosperous agricultural area of the country and two
hours by car from Vichy. Politically speaking, nothing ever happened there (the people of the Berry[14] were a calm lot), and con-
veniently, there was a strong concentration of militiamen and a
beautiful mansion that could be requisitioned. His mind was
made up, the owner's protests were ignored, and a few days later,
at the end of April, the four members of his family moved in,
alongside a dozen militiamen who would also take lodging there.

Simone is a small, dark-haired woman whose resolute gaze en-
livens a rather plain face. A teacher, married for eleven years, she
has followed her husband in both his geographical movements
and his ideological evolution; without being an active militia-
woman herself, she shares his convictions. At Saint-Amand she is
nevertheless reduced to the role of the dutiful wife and mother.
Bout de l'An had promised to be there the night before, June 5, for
the third birthday of their older son but was not. The younger son,
age six months, has a bad case of bronchitis, requiring much care.
In spite of this, and as is her habit, Simone goes at noon to the little restaurant nearby, escorted as always by two armed militiamen.
She leaves her children in the care of her mother-in-law. Few people in Saint-Amand are aware of her identity.

On this same day, Francis Bout de l'An is in Paris. He is not un-
happy; everyday he feels himself becoming more and more important. In this increasingly uncertain State that Vichy France has
become, the militia is one of the few undisputed forces, and Bout
de l'An is the political brains of the group. This great-grandson of
a public assistance foundling discovered on a December 31 and

14. Before being divided into departments, France was composed of regions (e.g., Bur-
gundy, Brittany, Normandy, and the like). The region in the center of France was the Berry.
In modern administrative terms, the Berry region is made up of two departments, the Cher
and the Indre.

therefore given the name Sylvestre Bout de l'An (end of the year) (Delperrié, 1:109) has followed a winding path. In the 1930s he was a militant member of the Action universitaire républicaine et socialiste and was close to the Communists. A trip to the U.S.S.R. made him change his mind and reoriented him toward fascism. After his university studies he taught history and geography, first in Tehran, then in Damascus. Returning to France in September 1941, he became one of the founders of the militia in 1943, assuming an ultracollaborationist stance. His dream is to create a great Nazi party, of which the militia would be the armed nucleus.

Darnand, less ideological than Bout de l'An, holds a somewhat different view; he prefers not to burn bridges with the national-ist—and thus potentially anti-German—sympathizers of Vichy. But he needs the former professor. Being himself a military man, a firebrand, a man of action, he is not entirely at ease in political discussions. Bout de l'An is just the opposite. Small and skinny, nearsighted to the point of being lost without his glasses, almost bald, and with a crooked nose, he can sound like a book when he talks. His rise through the ranks has been rapid. He was on the administrative staff of the militia at its founding and became its director of propaganda; in September 1943 he took the job of assistant secretary-general; in October of the same year, following Darnand, he joined the Waffen SS[15] (this was his victory of sorts over the traditionalist current). Bout de l'An's advancement was accelerated again in December 1943 when Darnand was named secretary-general for the maintenance of order and left the direction of the militia entirely to Bout de l'An. Bout de l'An will be even more independent after June 1944, when Darnand also becomes secretary-general of the interior. In the spring of 1944 he

15. During the summer of 1943 the Germans decided to create a French unit of the Waffen SS. To help in the recruitment of men for the unit, the Germans negotiated with Joseph Darnand and other leaders of the militia. In exchange for arms and permission to create militia training camps in twenty-one departments in the Southern Zone (formerly the Unoccupied Zone), Darnand joined the Waffen SS and helped to provide recruits from among his followers. The French unit eventually fought alongside the Germans in Russia, where they suffered heavy casualties.

eats lunch once a week with Prime Minister Laval (who would actually have preferred him as secretary-general in place of Darnand but did not dare appoint him); the two men, whose political paths have been similar, get along famously.

During the morning of June 6, Bout de l'An hears news of the Allied landing, but this does not worry him unduly. First, it is surely nothing more than a diversionary action, destined to turn attention away from the real operation site; and also, like most of his comrades, he has no doubts concerning the German military superiority and thus the outcome of the battle. He is equally calm on the personal level. His family is well protected, far from any possible front line, in that peaceful region of southern Berry, which is all the more pleasing to him for also being the region of his favorite literary hero, the Great Meaulnes[16]—one day, leading a detachment of militiamen, Bout de l'An even went to the école d'Epineuil-le-Fleuriel, in the Saint-Amand area, where Alain-Fournier studied. He thus calmly returns to Pigalle[17] that evening, to the hôtel Royal Navarin, which had been confiscated by the militia.

On the morning of June 6, the mayor of Saint-Amand, René Sadrin, gets into a car to go to a meeting in Bourges. Before the defeat, the mayor of Saint-Amand was Robert Lazurick, a Socialist deputy, lawyer, and journalist. After the establishment of the "French State,"[18] the former mayors were dismissed (in June 1940,

16. *Le Grand Meaulnes,* one of the most popular and successful French novels of this century, was published by Alain-Fournier in 1913. The hero, Augustin Meaulnes, is a romantic and adventurous adolescent who falls in love with a young woman he meets at a mysterious wedding party at a castle lost in the woods. He spends most of the rest of the novel trying to find his lost love with the help of a young admirer. Meaulnes is in fact a heroic and charismatic figure for most of the young boys at his school, exercising a near-mesmerizing influence over them. The novel has been translated into English as *The Wanderer.*

17. Pigalle, an area in the north of Paris at the foot of the Sacré Coeur church, has been Paris's most famous red-light district for many years.

18. The "French State" refers to the government of Vichy headed by Marshal Philippe Pétain. Pétain was voted full dictatorial powers by the National Assembly on July 10, 1944. Five hundred sixty-nine parliamentarians voted yes, and only eighty voted no. In this fashion the Third Republic voted itself out of existence. For a recent account of the vote, the events leading up to it, and the fate of those who voted against the establishment of the French State, see Pierre Miquel, *Les Quatre-vingts* (Paris: Fayard, 1995).

Lazurick was on board the *Massilia,* which was to take a group of French deputies to Africa),[19] and one of Lazurick's assistants, Maillaud, was named mayor in his place. However, it came to light several months later, in Vichy, that Maillaud himself was a Socialist and thus unsuitable. He is dismissed, and Sadrin is appointed in his place. Sadrin is also a former city councilman but one whose political past is in no way compromising. He is a man in his sixties, a veteran and former prisoner of war, a wine grower by profession. Before accepting his new job, Sadrin sets down certain conditions: he wants to be his own boss and will not tolerate the forced presence of overexcited *légionnaires.*[20] His politics during the war will consist of doing everything for the good of his citizens. The Resistance leaders like him, even if he is not one of them; he does not practice collaboration and helps them obtain false identity and food cards.

Sadrin arrives at Bourges at 9:30 A.M. Everything is quiet. He learned the news of the landing a little earlier, at Saint-Florent, but does not yet know what importance to give it. The meeting at the prefecture to which he was summoned unfolds as predicted; it is followed by a good meal, then by a small reception. The gathered mayors take a short walk in Bourges, where the streets are perfectly calm. They leave at about 6:00 P.M. and travel through peaceful small towns: Saint-Florent, Lunery, Châteauneuf, Dun. Sadrin is the last to be dropped off, and the car heads for Saint-Amand.

The Resistance members aware of a plan of insurrection are the only ones to be feverish on that day. Two of the leaders, Georges

19. In June 1940 members of the French government who wished to continue the fight against the Germans from France's colonies in North Africa boarded the *Massilia* and headed for Morocco. The *Massilia* docked in Casablanca on June 24, where the passengers, including Edouard Daladier, Georges Mandel, Jean Zay, and Yvon Delbos, received a cool reception from French authorities. Eventually branded as traitors, several of the passengers, including Daladier and Mandel, were tried for treason along with former premiers Léon Blum and Paul Reynaud at the abortive Riom trials organized by Vichy in 1942. Zay and Mandel were murdered by the militia in 1944.

20. The *légionnaires* were members of Vichy's veteran organization, the Légion des combattants, created in August 1940 to serve as activist supporters of Marshal Pétain and the new regime. Many members later joined the more militant Service d'ordre légionnaire, which evolved into the militia.

Chaillaud of Combat and an FTP member, go to the subprefecture. Chaillaud works for a sanitary installations company in Saint-Amand, but for some time now he has held a position at the subprefecture, where he was placed, with the approval of the Combat leadership, in order to perform various services. With the arrest of Subprefect Lecène, it is an office head, François Villatte, who, as of the previous night, is performing the duties of subprefect. He is an escaped prisoner of war whose sympathy for the Resistance is well known by Chaillaud. In their presence, Villatte calls Ardisson, commander of the First RF in Saint-Amand, to announce to him Chaillaud's visit. The two meet; already alerted on June 3 thanks to Colonel Bertrand, Ardisson confirms to the emissaries that, whatever happens, the soldiers under his command will not leave their barracks and will not intervene. Chaillaud takes the good news back to Van Gaver.

The FTP leaders rally their sympathizers throughout the whole department; they want to be present in force at Saint-Amand. In the area surrounding the town there are several independent maquis: Lalonnier and Diaz's Maupioux group, the First of May Company, the Gabriel Péri Company, the Yvan group—they all have to be informed and put under Lalonnier's command. Getting in contact with dozens of people, some of whom are hiding on isolated farms and others in the woods, takes time. Other Resistance fighters come from the region of Bourges.

The leaders of Combat also have a lot to do: above all, they must alert all the members of the movement that the day of open struggle has arrived. They succeed, more or less; however, many members are on the move or are unreachable and will not learn the news until that evening. Van Gaver is undoubtedly listening to his radio. Two speeches to the French people are heard, that of Eisenhower and that of de Gaulle. The first is broadcast by Radio London at 9:30 A.M. Eisenhower announces the Allied landing but remains rather vague concerning the role of the Resistance. "We must summon all our resources in order to expel the enemy from your country," he says, adding, "I am counting on your help for the crushing defeat of Hitler's Germany" (Aron, 70). There is no visible order for insurrection in these expressions, much less for the occupation of towns. De Gaulle addresses France at 5:30 P.M. His words are more belligerent: "For the sons of France, wherever they may be, whatever they may be, the simple, sacred duty is to fight with all the means at their disposal. It is a matter of destroying the enemy" (Aron, 149). Wherever they may be: thus, also at Saint-Amand. Through all means: why not insurrection? Destroy: kill. It is true that de Gaulle adds that the Resistance action must be coordinated with that of the Allied armies, but who wants to pay attention to these restrictions in the midst of general euphoria? In any case, at this particular time, Van Gaver is no longer there listening; the Resistance members are in the process of meeting at Clairins.

The Attack

At 6:00 P.M. at Clairins, a tiny little hamlet surrounding a lock on the canal of Berry, about seventy men gather. (General Intelligence, in its report of June 23, tries to inflate this number to justify the absence of all resistance on the part of the authorities: "700 to 800 individuals armed with machine guns and automatic rifles." After the war some Communist historians, to increase the importance of the event, affirm in turn, "200 fighters" [Guédin-Dreyfus, 211]. The participants themselves agree on the figure of seventy.) For the most part, they do not know each other: they come from different networks and do not all live in the same town. They proceed immediately to introductions, they tell each other the news of the insurrection that is setting all of France aglow, and they distribute weapons provided by the parachute drops for Combat to everyone lacking them, whether members of Combat or the FTP. While the arms distribution is going on, all vehicles arriving via this road are stopped. Then the Resistance members get into the trucks awaiting them, into private cars, and onto motorcycles and head for the nearby town. There, at 6:30 P.M., they join others from the FTP who were already armed and went there directly.

Lalonnier now takes command and divides his mix of troops into three groups of unequal size. The first, under the command of Van Gaver and Sochet, heads off to the subprefecture, where it meets with no resistance. Van Gaver sets himself up in the subprefect's office, announces he is taking over the duties of subprefect (Villatte's term has lasted only two days), and begins making phone calls. The others go next to the mayor's office, where they are welcomed with open arms, and to the police station. They get the same warm reception from the chief of police, Captain Cholet, who belongs to the Secret Army; but in order not to expose his Resistance affiliation too soon, they go about pretending to hold him in custody. Next they arrest, but with a show of consideration, two representatives of the Third Reich in Saint-Amand; they are the delegates to the bureau of the STO. The second group occupies the post office. There the Resistance fighters surprise a militiaman, Mathiot, who is so severely clubbed that he is left for dead. Discreet roadblocks are set up around the entrances to the town, and at 7:00 P.M. the control post on the road to Bourges reports the appearance of an enemy worthy of the name. A private car has just passed it with two well-known militiamen inside, Jean Parmène and Joseph Patin, and they have machine guns in the backseat. The Resistance fighters stop them downtown, make them get out of their vehicle, take away their weapons, and lead them to the monument to the dead. By 7:15, Parmène and Patin have been shot to death; their bodies will remain there until the next morning.

On June 6 the insurgents' main enemy, as well as the immediate one, is not the Germans. To begin with, there never really were any in Saint-Amand. In 1940 the Demarcation Line ran north of the town, and even after 1942 and the invasion of the "Free Zone," there were armed forces only in the big towns, Bourges and Montluçon. In Saint-Amand there are only a few government workers, who are not very visible—a large portion of the population will see Germans for the first time in 1944, at the time of the Wehrmacht's retreat. Moreover, the Germans are not an adversary on equal footing. The real enemy is the militiamen. They are seen in great numbers, many of them are known from schooldays spent together or because they belong to one's own family, and there are good reasons to detest them. They have declared war on the Resistance fighters; they arrest them, torture them, and kill them, or else they denounce them to the German police (the Gestapo), who do the same thing or sometimes deport them. These very young men—most of them are twenty to twenty-five years old—pride themselves on being toughs; one team of them from Saint-Amand will take the name "the Killers." The Communists are the militiamen's first target (but it is true that they call any person guilty of resistance a Communist); when they trouble themselves with ideological considerations, they like to present themselves as the white knights of that noble cause, anticommunism. Beating an arrested Resistance fighter until he bleeds, one of the militiamen of Saint-Amand roars at him, "You want red; I'll give you red."

The Communists feel the same hatred in return. The instructions sent out by the high command of the FTP Southern Zone on June 6 contain the following orders: "Exterminate all the Kraut garrisons and all the militiamen of the Darnand Waffen SS; . . . kill without mercy the murderers and bastards of the militia, everywhere you find them" (Guingouin, 178). The term "exterminate" is not chosen at random; these enemies are just barely human. It is not a matter of pondering the individual guilt of each one; the very fact that they are in the militia is sufficient reason to condemn them to death. In war you just do not ask yourself if the soldier facing you deserves a bullet or not.

This is why the main group of resisters, comprising the fiercest fighters of the FTP and led by Lalonnier himself with Blanchard second in command, heads to the office of the militia. Finally, they will be able to do battle with their enemies, they will fight on equal terms, they will show what they are worth! The "siege" of the militia begins at 7:00 P.M. Actually, it is more a demonstration of a lack of military experience on both sides. The resisters, whose numbers are greater, surround the building and shoot at it, but their bullets hit no one. The militiamen retaliate, with the same result, until the moment when a stray bullet kills a person passing by who has nothing to do with the attack. They also throw some grenades, one of which destroys the machine gun in Lalonnier's hands and slightly wounds the person next to him. Simone Bout de l'An, shocked by the pitiful military efficiency of her defenders, commands them to resist more forcefully.

Then, little by little, things change. One of the two *chefs de trentaine*, Clément Marchand, a Parisian hotel page who ended up in the militia at Saint-Amand, decides to attempt a breakout. He slips on a beige, fur-lined jacket and goes out a back window overlooking the gardens that border the Marmande. To his great surprise, this is not really a siege at all: there is no one on this side of the mansion to stop him. He thus continues to flee and "requisitions" a motor scooter, which enables him to go to the militia buildings in Sancoins. Marchand and the local chief telephone Bourges. From there, the bad news is immediately transmitted to Vichy, then to Paris and the German command. It seems that, to better justify his fleeing, Marchand reported American, British, Canadian, and French paratroopers who were supposedly dropped over Saint-Amand.

But inside the mansion in which the militia is staying, hope for a satisfactory solution is beginning to fade. Simone thus turns to Bastide, the other *chef de trentaine* who has remained there, and urges him to start negotiations with the attackers; the family is in no condition to endure a prolonged siege; her sick little boy needs special care. Bastide contacts the resisters by phone. He informs them that there are women and children with them, and he proposes that the militiamen give themselves up, on condition that their safety be assured. Lalonnier accepts, not intending to keep his word. Promises made to the enemy are worthless; they are part of the ruses of war. Simone hangs a white flag from the window.

Having thrown down their weapons and put their hands up, the eight militiamen leave the building one after another at about 11:00 P.M., followed by the two women and the two children. Simone proudly states her identity. The name Bout de l'An is not unknown to the Resistance fighters. What are they going to do with these prisoners? Lalonnier favors the expedient measure recommended by the FTP and already used to settle the case of Parmène and Patin: put their backs to the wall and shoot them dead. But Blanchard, who has participated in the siege at Lalonnier's side, finds such an action unacceptable. They consult Van Gaver, who is of the same opinion as Blanchard: since the militiamen have given themselves up, they must be treated as prisoners of war. Besides, the Resistance fighters would first have to interrogate them and then condemn them only with full knowledge of the facts. Lalonnier, who does not want to cause dissension between Resistance groups, gives in, but says to Blanchard, "Since that's how it's going to be, you take the militiamen, I wash my hands of them" (Delperrié, 2:97). So they are all taken to the subprefecture.

Would it be right to blame Blanchard for having interceded in order to spare these lives, to make a little more justice and humanity prevail? Certainly not. It is precisely at this moment, however, in this perfectly benevolent gesture, that the tragic fate of the various actors in this drama is sealed.

In their confusion, the besieged leave the premises without destroying the files and, in particular, the list of names of all the militiamen in the region, along with their addresses. The triumphant Resistance fighters who are occupying the building take the list and soon launch a manhunt, in town and in the neighboring villages, that will continue the next day. The number of persons arrested climbs rapidly. What to do with them? Saint-Amand has no prison. Van Gaver, the new subprefect, decides to ask Mayor René Sadrin to help.

On the outskirts of Saint-Amand, Sadrin passed the patrols of the First RF, who quickly informed him of the situation. Back home now, he receives a phone call from Van Gaver, who asks him if there is not a room at the town hall where they could keep the prisoners for the night. Sadrin honors his request, then expresses his surprise at the upheaval that has occurred at Saint-Amand. "What, isn't Bourges occupied too?" Van Gaver asks. No, everywhere else, it's calm as can be. "And you weren't bothered on the way?" The roads have never been so peaceful (Sadrin, 17).

Preparation to Retaliate

In the early morning hours of June 7, Francis Bout de l'An is awakened in his Pigalle hotel by the militiaman on duty. "Bad news, boss. The terrorists have taken Saint-Amand, your family is in their custody" (Delperrié, 2:97).

Bout de l'An jumps out of bed, calls Vichy, and sees Darnand, who is also in Paris and who assures him that all the forces of the militia are at his disposal. He calls three comrades and leaves with them by car for Saint-Amand. But on the way he realizes that the four of them alone will not be able to "liberate" the town, and they thus make a turn in the direction of Vichy to seek reinforcements. Once in Vichy, they phone the subprefecture of Saint-Amand, and Van Gaver answers. A comical conversation ensues, giving rise to an escalation of threats.

In Moulins the commander of the German armed forces was informed of events in the course of the night. He lets Bout de l'An know that they will intercede the following night. In the afternoon of the same day they send reconnaissance planes over the town to collect all the necessary information.

In the evening, Bout de l'An leaves Vichy, heading a unit of about thirty militiamen, Marchand and Auguste Vigier among them. The latter is the principal ringleader of the militia in the region. It is therefore at his house that Bout de l'An spends the night of June 7–8, waiting to go into Saint-Amand on the heels of the German army.

Brief Triumph

Their victory confirmed, the leaders of the Resistance must now learn how to manage their success. The new subprefect, Van Gaver, will have to resolve the problem of the prisoners as soon as possible; in the meantime their number has grown. He has obtained authorization from René Sadrin to put them in the town hall, where they are divided into three groups. The mother of Bout de l'An and his two children are sent to the hospital (this place is all the more suitable in that the little one is still ill), so in fact they are released. The men are locked in the cellar of the town hall, and six women arrested during the night are placed under guard in the marriage hall. Simone is also detained there despite her protests at being separated from her children.

Why was first sorting process carried out, why was Simone put on one side and her children and mother-in-law on the other? Because burdened with these unexpected prisoners, Van Gaver and Blanchard decided to make political and military use of them as hostages. In the minds of the French, this practice is associated with the German occupier, who in this way punishes the civilian population for any aggression wrought against German nationals. But the Resistance fighters decide not to be mindful of their means, for everything is acceptable as long as it contributes to victory, including the enemy's methods. However, Bout de l'An's children are too young—detaining them and using them could provoke a feeling of repulsion in the population—and his mother is an elderly woman. His wife, on the other hand, is in the prime of life and, furthermore, does not hide her hostility toward the resisters. She is therefore well suited for the role of hostage. To convince themselves that the steps they are taking are justified, the resisters tell each other that Simone is "Darnand's mistress," which is probably untrue.

As for Lalonnier, he does not have these worries. Relieved of the prisoners, he leaves Saint-Amand on a truck when evening comes. He travels the surrounding areas, alerting all his sympathizers about the events that have just occurred and calling them together for the next day in Saint-Amand. During the night, Sochet and Blanchard, who have stayed in town, go to the depot, where hunting rifles requisitioned at the beginning of the Occupation had been stored, and transport them to the prefecture. Elsewhere, resisters seriously wound one of their own comrades by mistake.

On the morning of June 7 the weather is glorious. It is a Wednesday, but nobody thinks of going to work; their sudden freedom calls for a celebration. Many stores are closed, yet the farmers who have come to town to do their shopping (Saint-Amand is an active commercial center) do not mind at all. At the subprefecture, a barrel of wine is tapped first thing in the morning, and everyone helps himself to plenty. A box of tobacco, another rare commodity, is opened for use by the free citizens of Saint-Amand. Vehicles and food are requisitioned in exchange for coupons that will be honored by the future government. Posters are put up in town announcing general mobilization and urging young men to join the army of Free France; at the Rex movie theater, which has been put at the disposal of the insurgents by its owner, Van Gaver (the past weekend, *Les Roquevillards*, with Charles Vanel, was playing), they are recruiting and liberally distributing the recovered shotguns. There are also some more modern weapons that the British dropped to them by parachute. But the machine guns are much too greased up; they will have to be cleaned first. And the Sten submachine guns prove to be too dangerous—the slightest touch makes them go off. A demobilized teacher remembers having gone to the subprefecture on that morning: "When I saw that they were giving you a shotgun with no shoulder strap and three cartridges per person, I went back home." Nevertheless, the number of volunteers multiplies; there will soon be almost three hundred, four times more than the night before. They willingly tell each other encouraging news: the Allies also have landed in Marseilles and Sète, the Resistance has taken Limoges, Bourges is surrounded, Montluçon is shaky.

Everyone is giving orders, for there really is no one single command. Van Gaver now sits in the subprefect's seat, but his is a power suited to peacetime, not to revolution; and not being an authoritarian sort of man, he is willing to hold discussions with this group and that group. Lalonnier commands from his position; Sochet, from his. The fusion of Combat and the FTP is too recent for them truly to form a single entity, even though there is not too much friction between them; each man appeals spontaneously to the leaders he knows.

Who, in fact, joins the FFI that morning? Basically, young men dodging the draft into the STO who have not done their military service and therefore have no war experience but who are itching to show the Germans that they are capable of doing battle with them. One of these new recruits deserves special mention. In 1943 the members of a first Resistance network, Libération-Sud, were arrested. Rightly or wrongly, a certain individual was suspected of having betrayed them. Since nothing was ever proved against him, I will not name this individual, certain traits of whom are perhaps pure fantasy. I will designate him by this conventional appellation, the Traitor. A Jew, he became engaged in Resistance activities early on, but it seems he was arrested by the Gestapo and "sent back," and afterward he furnished useful information to both sides. Before June 6 the Resistance fighters of Saint-Amand, who suspected him without being absolutely certain, kept him on the sidelines and did not let him participate in any action. But on the morning of June 7 he is among the first to sign up. Upon leaving the sub-prefecture, he meets Chaillaud and says very calmly, tapping him on the shoulder, "You know, you wouldn't have me in the Resistance; well, now I'm in it."

Now masters of the town, the resisters face numerous issues that demand their attention. A third German, who works at the railroad office, is arrested. In Saint-Amand, as in the surrounding areas, some continue to track down militiamen or those assumed to be militiamen. They arrest a good number of them and take them to the cellar of the town hall; but others, whose identity they do not know, stay among them and do their best to record everything in their memories. It should not be assumed that these arrests are carried out with much rigor. A witness reports: "Two guys enter the Berthomie Hotel waving revolvers, asking if there aren't some militiamen there; the proprietress says no, everyone present assures them of their sympathy, and that is enough for them. Everyone shakes hands, and they leave without having searched the hotel or asked for identity papers" (Archives Nationales, A.IV.8).

A group of Resistance members from Combat under the direction of Georges Le Quellec, one of Van Gaver's lieutenants, devotes itself to implementing the Green Plan, that is to say, the destruction of the railways: on the Bourges line, north of Saint-Amand, two locomotives are sent crashing into each other, their drivers having jumped out beforehand. Others requisition things for their own purposes; a truckload of tires leaves town for an unknown destination. Nobody really watches the entrances and exits to the town—André Rochelet, a militia leader unknown to the resisters, can quietly take the train to Bourges during the morning. No one thinks to camouflage requisitioned vehicles. Summarizing the situation, one former Resistance fighter laments, "It was a mess; we needed a leader." As for the police force, which does not know whose side to take, it tries to maintain a semblance of order and limit the damage. It protects "certain stores, with the aim of avoiding a round of looting already underway," and as the secretary of police adds in his report of June 17, "With numerous armed individuals being found in a nearly intoxicated state, I succeed at about 4:00 P.M. in obtaining the order to close all drinking establishments." (What a brave officer!)

But if euphoria reigns in the streets, it is a different story at the subprefect's office. The news piles up on Van Gaver's desk, merciless news: in the Cher neither Bourges nor Vierzon has stirred, and in the nearby Allier region Moulins and Montluçon alike have remained calm. It is still believed that in the wake of the Allied landing, the German empire is faltering, but fear of enemy reprisal is beginning to grow. What should be done? Opinions differ, and all of them are followed in some way, all at the same time. Intolerantly positive, Sochet declares that it is possible to hold the town; is it not a matter of only a few days? Is not all of France in the process of waking up and mobilizing its formidable forces? They must dig trenches to block certain roads and cut down trees (the only victims of the morning) along the Berry canal, as if tree trunks could stop tanks. Van Gaver and Blanchard recall that it had never been a question of engaging in open combat, but they still hope that it will be possible to hold their own in town without having to fight.

They also begin to anticipate to what use they can put the burdensome gift they have received, the militiamen and the Bout de l'An family. It dawns on them to make hostages of the prisoners. As the afternoon begins and Van Gaver speaks by phone to the leaders of the militia in Vichy, he threatens them: "We are holding the Bout de l'An family, and if you attack us, we'll blow everything up" (Delperrié, 2:98). By that, he no doubt means that the hostages will be executed. But will this threat, which carries meaning with the militiamen, be enough to prevent the occupation of Saint-Amand by the German army (assuming, of course, that it still has the strength for it after the terrible blow it took from the Allied landing)? The fact remains that this initiative is taken seriously enough to justify the hasty printing of a poster put up on town walls, written as follows (it is significant that it addresses the other militiamen, not the Germans):

NOTICE

We have taken as prisoners thirty-six militia members, both women and men. Let it be known that if any militia members from elsewhere take reprisal against Saint-Amand, the hostages will be shot to death.

The Committee for Resistance
(Delalande, 19)

So now the prisoners are officially transformed into hostages ready for execution. But at the same time, keeping them in Saint-Amand is not safe enough. At about 1:00 P.M. they are taken out of the town hall and led to the trucks awaiting them. Simone is allowed a quick visit with her children at the hospital. The prisoners who pass between the rows of onlookers are booed mightily. The populace is only too happy to prove that it can tell who is good and who is bad; it hurries to make up for the four years that have gone by since the collapse. The prisoners get into the trucks. Le Quellec and other armed Resistance fighters surround them. They go to Maupioux, to Lalonnier's old hideout; but once there, Le Quellec sees that the place is not well enough equipped to be a clandestine prison. They thus return to Saint-Amand. On the way, Le Quellec and Simone rail against each other: according to Le Quellec, all the bad comes from the militiamen; according to Simone, from the "terrorists." Once they have returned to the town hall, they find themselves back in the cellar or the marriage hall.

In the meantime, something eventful has taken place in Saint-Amand: a reconnaissance plane flying at low altitude and marked with a swastika has lingered over the town. Not all the Germans have been annihilated after all. The effect on the crowd is stunning: the very same people who a short while before were speaking proudly of their victory now rush back home to pack a small bag and leave town before the Germans retaliate.

After Le Quellec's return at almost 6:00 P.M., all the Resistance leaders meet. This time the military men have their say, and the politicians have to follow; Lalonnier assumes the command of what is now called the Cher group. They evaluate the situation. Things have not unfolded exactly as they had imagined. The night before, a militiaman (Marchand) escaped; had he not been able to escape, the alert would not have been given. The other large towns in the area have not risen up; if only they had done so, the Germans would not have known which way to turn and would have left Saint-Amand alone. A German plane has been spotted; in spite of the Allied landing, the Germans have not all surrendered. The police of Charenton, a town on the road to Sancoins, have just phoned; they warn of the arrival of military forces. Conclusion: the German army will return, and the resisters, however courageous they may be, are in no condition to hold the town; they must therefore fall back on their alternative solution: evacuation and escape into the maquis. They will first regroup in Châteaumeillant, about thirty kilometers southwest of Saint-Amand, then go on through Guéret, also said to be in Resistance hands, and from there they will go into the woods of the Creuse. The militiamen are taken along, escorted by the people from Combat. They have to leave during the night. The signal to depart will be a drumroll.

Certain FTP members, like Diaz, nevertheless choose to stay and hide in the area. Blanchard and his brother-in-law, Sagnelonge, who have not slept a wink the past two nights, are sent home to catch up on a little sleep. They will be alerted when the time comes.

The Departure

A good number of Resistance fighters have assembled at the Rex. It is there, on the place Carré, that the trucks that are to transport them are grouped. Platoons are formed, and each one takes its turn boarding a truck. The prisoners, accompanied by an escort group, are also led here from the town hall. Exactly how many of them are there? Accounts vary on this point. According to some, there are thirteen men and six women; according to others, there are more. The most realistic figure seems to be twenty-five in all, of whom seven are women. Since the posters mentioned thirty-six militiamen, what became of the others? Delalande, whose account is in general very precise, says that a few had been forgotten in the town hall cellars, along with the three Germans also left behind (p. 18); a report at the subprefecture dated 25 July 1944 speaks of a group of ten prisoners freed by the German army (Archives départmentales, Z.1555). The Resistance veterans mention a preliminary investigation of sorts, at the end of which they are said to have detained only "those who had the worst reputations" (but then they are still going only by hearsay) and the women.

Some prisoners owe their release to pure chance. One of the resisters recognizes a neighbor from his village among the prisoners and asks, "Why are you here?" to which the answer is "I have no idea. I was simply arrested." The resister makes some inquiries and finds out that the neighbor was mistaken for another man by the same name who, indeed, was an actual militiaman—the arrests are made on the basis of the lists seized the night before. The false militiaman thus gets out of the truck and, gushing with gratitude, goes back home. The others remain there, pale-faced.

As for the women, it becomes fairly obvious at this time that they are not fierce militiawomen but rather the sometimes strictly temporary girlfriends of the militiamen, arrested at the same time as the men, in the course of nocturnal searches. But in this context of masculine confrontation, giving amorous preference to the enemy is already a crime in itself, a betrayal of the homeland, even if these women's choice was dictated by the material advantages they stood to gain rather than by ideological sympathies. Standing in front of the trucks, their hearts sink. Several weep unabashedly, and cheap makeup streams down their cheeks. "Sleeparounds," observes one of the resisters (Perrot, 24). Perhaps not meriting imprisonment, the so-called militiawomen are nevertheless taken along, for it is thought that they, as much as Simone, have a higher exchange value than the men. Simone herself is disturbed at being put into the same category as these women of little virtue. Stiff and silent, she has seated herself in the truck, and she glances scornfully at her less than dignified companions.

The trucks leave one after another between 10:00 P.M. and 1:00 in the morning. They take the Cher bridge and head toward Châteaumeillant. Blanchard was awakened only at midnight and ran to catch one of the last trucks. The person who was supposed to wake up Sagnelonge never showed up at his house. Asleep at the town hall, two resisters in the group guarding the militiamen are also overlooked.

They are far from being the only ones left behind, but not all the forgotten are asleep. Along with eight comrades and his own truck, equipped with wood for the gasogene[21] and a demijohn of red wine for the men, François Briandet stands on the road to Charenton, which, although he is unarmed, he is supposed to monitor. They have been told to wait for the sound of the drum. Night falls, and still there is nothing (a cyclist is said to have passed by with the drum, but almost no one heard him). They decide to send a scout to the subprefecture. The scout travels there on bicycle and finds all its lights on but no one inside. He notices a gun and takes it back to the friends waiting for him. What to do? They engage in a discussion. One of them proposes that they hide in the forest of Meillant; another proposes the forest of Tronçais. But Briandet brings them around to his opinion: "I know a butcher in the Resistance at Châteaumeillant. Let's go see him." Why not? They leave, stop along the way, and arrive in Châteaumeillant, where—miraculously—they meet up again

21. During the war the gasoline shortage resulted in the development of substitute energy sources. Gasogene engines, which burned wood instead of gasoline, were widely installed in cars and trucks.

with their comrades. Some of them take off by their own means for Culan or Lignières.

In the darkness they cannot always distinguish their own men from the others, and their nerves begin to fray. The first Resistance fighter to be killed is shot by his comrades, who thought they saw an enemy.

In the early hours of the morning a regrouping has nevertheless been carried out in Châteaumeillant. At this juncture an incomprehensible episode occurs: most, if not all, of the trucks return to Saint-Amand. Why? It would seem that at this time the Resistance fighters received a telephone message telling them that it was all a false alarm and that they could come back to town. The message is said to have been sent by the Traitor. The news is in line with their hopes: they were wrong to have become frightened and left too soon. The trucks therefore return to town, but several hundred meters before the bridge, they are stopped by a car whose occupants confirm to them that the German army is indeed in the process of entering into Saint-Amand, from the opposite side. It is already daylight when the trucks, having turned around, again leave for Châteaumeillant. Moreover, not everyone leaves, as certain Resistance fighters have entered Saint-Amand without being intercepted and will leave only when they hear the first shots fired. No longer knowing where their comrades are, they will hide for several days in the nearby forest of Habert before rejoining the others.

The Retreat

The trucks pass Châteaumeillant this time, then La Châtre, and they stop in the village of Bonnat on the road to Guéret. Here they take a little rest, count their numbers, and regroup. Some food is distributed. The hostages remain on board the trucks. The villagers come forth, suspicious at first, then joyful to learn that the

Liberation is under way: "We'll get those Krauts!" Late in the afternoon everyone gets back in the trucks, and in the evening they
arrive in Guéret, the prefecture of the Creuse region.

On the evening of June 8 the town of Guéret is in smoke and
flames. The events that have unfolded there since June 6 are like
those at Saint-Amand (minus the hostages). "François," a teacher
who directs the MUR and the FFI of the Creuse, wants uncondi-
tionally to pass for a hard-liner: he is intransigent with collaborators, intolerant toward the FTP, and uncompromising with his
own subordinates. The occupation of the town here is complicat-
ed by the presence of the école de la Garde (the training school
for the Garde mobile, the antiriot police, which is a military
force). A part of its officers opposes the "François" project; another part supports it. On June 7 fighting takes place throughout the
town, the resisters braving the German garrison and the militiamen. The German soldiers surrender; they will be imprisoned but
will be subjected to no ill treatment. The militiamen defend
themselves, then capitulate after several hours and are also locked
up. Other collaborators are pursued and imprisoned. In the morning of June 8 a German company attempts to retake the town but
is driven back. New encounters take place in town with militia
members who were not captured the night before. The local newspaper building is on fire. In the evening, in retaliation for the at-
tacks they withstand, the Resistance fighters execute three imprisoned militiamen.

When the trucks from Saint-Amand arrive at the edge of town,
they are welcomed by the local Resistance members. The prisoners are led to the prison, and the Resistance fighters from Saint-
Amand go to the école de la Garde to spend the night in the barracks there, not hesitating to take a few shots at some militiamen
whom they think they spot. The night is short; they remain on the
alert and sleep next to the trucks. On the morning of June 9 they
are hoping for a respite, and several of them are sitting at a table
in a café waiting to be served, when suddenly a German plane flies

over the town and begins machine-gunning them. Lalonnier gives the order for immediate departure; they have not had the time to get the gasogenes working, so the trucks must be towed. From his position, "François" (who is directing the resistance in the Creuse and thus, indirectly, the refugees from Saint-Amand) also orders the evacuation of the town, but he "forgets" to alert the FTP, whose members will blame him for a long time to come for this "absent-mindedness."

The line of trucks moves off toward the south. The convoy is pelted with gunfire by German planes, but there are no casualties. Inside the trucks, no one knows where they are going, including the drivers—the kilometer markers have been smeared with tar to impede the movements of German soldiers in the region. Anxiety mounts in the new recruits as what began as a game takes a serious turn. One of the volunteers holds forth as follows: "Well, old friend, you talk about a story. The night before last I leave the wife, the kid and the mother-in-law to go to the Rex to see what's going on. Like my buddies, and because I don't like the Krauts and those bastards the militiamen, I join in to liberate Saint-Amand. And now here I am in the Creuse two days later! Oh, good God almighty. For a story, this is some story. I'm telling you, sonny, stories like this give me the shivers" (Perrot, 33).

As the afternoon begins, the trucks, having followed some very winding, bumpy roads, make a stop in a very small town. The sign at the entrance of the village reads "Bosmoreau-les-Mines." The vehicles are hidden under some branches to make them invisible to planes, Lalonnier summons all those in charge to come to him, and a long discussion begins. Now what do they do? After exchanging some spirited arguments, all agree that the group is too big, too visible, and too vulnerable; that it is therefore better to divide in two. The whole next day will be devoted to this splitting up, and on the day after that, June 11, each group will occupy its temporary quarters.

Before it is able to go to bed for the night, the platoon in charge of the prisoners must confront an unforeseen problem: one of the young women is feeling poorly. It soon becomes apparent that she is in the process of having a miscarriage. The jolting of the truck has gotten the better of her ill-attached baby. Panic ensues: these young men do not know how to handle the situation. They appeal to Simone, who overcomes her animosity toward the women and takes the matter into her own hands. Two militiamen are sent to get water; the young woman is taken care of and calmed down. They all fall asleep.

German Repression

During the night of June 7–8 a battalion of the 1000th security regiment of the Jesser Brigade has taken position on the outskirts of Saint-Amand. The German troops form a semicircle, leaving open the road to the west (the Cher bridge). Why do they fail to make a full circle when they are already in place to do so? Everything indicates that they would prefer that the enemy leave in order to avoid a head-on clash. Could it be that they have overestimated the military power of the Resistance fighters, the efficiency of the "terrorists"?

On June 8, at around 5:00 A.M., the German soldiers enter town dressed for combat, which makes a big impression on the townspeople: blackened faces, helmets covered with foliage (even though they are in town), patches of yellow and green on their camouflage uniforms. They are accompanied by armored cars and light tanks, and they shoot at anything that moves. The trenches dug the night before and the trees that were cut down fail to slow their advance at all. They meet with no resistance, and their sole casualty hurts himself by falling off a bicycle. They knock on doors on the streets where they pass and arrest whomever they happen to come across: they need guilty parties. The police station prudently raises a white flag.

The German soldiers are guided by a few French militiamen; at their head are Le Lanchon and Mathiot. The latter was left for dead at the post office on June 6 but has recovered and now wants vengeance. Following their indications, the searches by the German soldiers become more specific. They arrest persons suspected of sympathizing with the Resistance or individuals who have the misfortune of displeasing them, and they pack them into the offices of the subprefecture, nearly two hundred people in all. The first victims are killed, a group numbering five: passersby struck by chance, those who moved too slowly or too fast.

What are the town officials doing during this time? In the middle of the night, Villatte chose not to leave with the Resistance fighters, and they have thus locked him up in a room of the subprefecture, along with another office head and those in command of the police force, to make it look as if he is being held by force. "Liberated" by the soldiers, he resumes his duties as a replacement for the subprefect and tries to intervene to effect appeasement, negotiations, and the release of certain prisoners. Sadrin, who speaks good German from having been a prisoner of war in Germany for five years, also tries to intervene. An officer rebuffs him sharply and sends him back home after letting him know that the army has at its disposal detailed information, photographs, and reports concerning what happened the night before. On the road back, Sadrin passes a few individuals with weapons but without uniforms, individuals whom he takes for Resistance fighters and to whom he shouts, "The Krauts are in front of the town hall, hide!" They reply, triumphant, "Those are our friends, Saint-Amand is ours!" (Sadrin, 190). A disastrous error: they were militiamen. Sadrin manages to get back home anyway.

André Sagnelonge is awakened by gunshots at 7:00 A.M., for no one has come to alert Blanchard's brother-in-law of the departure of the maquisards. He thinks there is a struggle going on in the street, slips on his clothes, to which he proudly attached an FFI tricolored armband the night before, and grabs his gun. Young

René Girardhello, age sixteen, who idolizes him and follows him everywhere, jumps up to his side. The two men rush into the street. Recognizing his error, Sagnelonge throws down his gun, but it is too late. They find themselves eyeball to eyeball with the German soldiers who, upon seeing their armbands, arrest them and lead them off with the other prisoners. First, they are lined up against a wall, with their hands up; they wait to be executed. Then they hear another order and can put their hands down. The captain of the police force, Cholet, in charge of verifying their identity, hopes to work things out.

Sagnelonge, who only now is beginning to comprehend the situation, immediately thinks of his brother-in-law and asks his neighbor, "Was Blanchard able to get away?" Learning that such was the case, he decides to try his luck and attempt to run away. He participated too openly in the insurrection of the night before to hope to be released, and furthermore, his armband is damning evidence against him. It must be said that he is very experienced when it comes to escaping: taken as a prisoner of war in Germany in 1940, he escaped five times, from stricter and stricter internment camps, getting recaptured each time before succeeding the sixth time, in 1942. Once in Saint-Amand he immediately sought to carry out resistance activity. He has great admiration for Blanchard, who is younger and more cultivated than he is. As soon as he sees the German soldier turn his head, he jumps over the fence and starts running; Girardhello rushes after him. Unfortunately, the soldier hears them, turns around, and fires. The two men are killed instantly. Captain Cholet tries to intervene, and a stray bullet strikes him in the head.

The German soldiers do not content themselves with shooting at random but pick out a few armed resisters; three other persons meet their death fighting. On their side, the militiamen are jubilant over a good catch: one of the resisters' small trucks, out looking for fuel for the gasogenes, was delayed in town that morning; the occupants were recognized, disarmed, and locked up. At 3:00

P.M. they are led to a garden next door. To the seven resisters, Le Lanchon has added Marcel Roger, an old pal with whom he attended youth camp but against whom he is nursing a serious grudge: Roger has always refused to follow him into the militia. Arrested that morning, he will pay dearly for his stubbornness. At 3:15 P.M. the eight men are executed; their bodies will remain on site until that evening.

The Germans also investigate the First RF, whose soldiers did not intervene the night before: why? The guilty party must be found. Mathiot arrests Colonel Larouquette, a retired officer, whom he believes to be a Freemason; that is enough to condemn him. Commander Ardisson is put under arrest and later will be sent to Bourges. There is talk of disarming and disbanding the regiment.

A shot rings out, fired by mistake by a militiaman. But the German rapid deployment force, on the lookout, is convinced that some terrorists have fired on them. To rest assured, they burn the downtown area with flamethrowers and incendiary grenades. They prevent the firefighters who arrive on the scene from intervening. Early that afternoon, another German column enters town from the road to Montluçon. Following a misunderstanding, a new round of shooting breaks out. Some German planes fly over the town at low altitude. One of them makes a false maneuver and touches a treetop. The plane crashes, setting off a new fire, and its pilot is killed. Everywhere the tension is extreme; the townspeople are convinced that the town will be bombarded during the night.

The German repression, carried out with the help of the militia, brings about the death of nineteen people on this day of June 8; nearly two hundred are locked up in the camp of the First RF and at the post office; six houses are burned. All the weight of the repression falls on the civilian population. As one of the inhabitants of the town says the next day, "On June 7, the maquis ordered the rounds of drinks and, on June 8, it left us the job of paying the check" (Sadrin, 180).

The Militia's Revenge

At Sancoins, Francis Bout de l'An, Vigier, Marchand, and the other militiamen have waited for the German troops to free the road for them. They arrive in Saint-Amand late in the morning and observe the damage already incurred. Bout de l'An learns that his family is at the hospital; he goes there and finds his mother and two children. They will be moved out, toward Vichy, in the afternoon. He demands an explanation from Ardisson, who justifies his nonintervention by saying that he is not there to fight the maquis. Finally, Bout de l'An goes to the subprefecture. Once again Villatte must give up exercising the functions of subprefect, and this time it is Vigier who supplants him; his second in command will have the upper hand over the police. As of this moment and until they leave in August, the militiamen will run the town.

Their first initiative will be to engage in a methodical manhunt of their own: all those who escaped the arrests carried out by the Resistance fighters on June 7 engage in a chase in the opposite direction on June 8. Instead of individuals chosen randomly by the Germans, resisters, members of their families, and sympathizers — about sixty persons in all — are arrested one after another. The militiamen pillage the homes of the absent Resistance members, in particular Van Gaver's, and they attempt to set fire to the Rex movie theater, which served as a recruiting station the night before; but the intervention by one of the Germans from the STO office, just recently released, makes them temporarily abandon their plan.

The next morning, June 9, Bout de l'An makes an attempt to find his wife. He has been told about the trip to Maupioux during the afternoon of June 7 (but not about the prisoners' return). He takes his militiamen and has a few German soldiers go with him. They go directly to Lalonnier's hideout, the forester warden's house. Soldiers and militiamen storm the place; bullets rain down on the silent house. Inside, the warden and his family are lying on the floor, praying to God for protection. Bout de l'An goes into the house and interrogates the warden, who knows nothing; however, while rummaging around, he finds some objects and some papers belonging to the arrested militiamen, which were left behind. The warden is severely beaten, but he is still just as unable to furnish the slightest information. The group therefore abandons him and returns to Saint-Amand, which Bout de l'An leaves once again for Vichy, after leaving Vigier in charge of handling all affairs.

On this same morning of June 9, René Sadrin has asked for an appointment with Vigier. He wants to plead the case of the hostages and has decided to approach him from what he thinks is the vantage point of Vigier's vulnerability: Vigier comes from this very region, the Berry, and in a small locality everyone knows everyone else. Sadrin was present at the recent marriage of Vigier's brother. He is received promptly by the new subprefect. The subprefecture is full of militiamen, over whom Marchand reigns; Sadrin knows only a few of them. He therefore attempts to play on his interlocutor's feelings for their beloved Berry: the town had nothing to do with what just happened; why punish it for what it merely was subjected to? Couldn't Vigier speak with the German authorities to arrange the release of those unjustly imprisoned?

Vigier first replies that the authorities in question have put the prisoners back in the hands of the militia, which is to say, back into his own hands. This means those authorities consider the matter closed. Noting that their countrymen, the three administrative officials, are unhurt (as opposed to what happened at the same time in Tulle), they decide that the town has been sufficiently punished. If the Resistance fighters had not taken hostages, the matter would have been settled with that. But the German soldiers know that the militia was more seriously affected: they therefore turn over control of the prisoners to them so that they may do with them as they wish. The resisters took hostages to protect themselves against retaliation, and yet it is precisely for this action, not for the insurrection, that they bring retaliation upon themselves.

In other respects, Vigier appears sensitive to Sadrin's arguments, but he introduces a distinction. On one side are the leaders of the insurrection (he too is thinking of Larouquette) or those who were captured with weapons in their hands; releasing them is out of the question. On the other side are the family members of the resisters and the sympathizers; for them, some agreement can be reached. Vigier has a complete list of the prisoners drawn up. In the afternoon the prisoners' family members visit Sadrin and beg him to intervene on their behalf. He returns to see Vigier and, with an inspector of schools who has come to plead the case of a few teachers, ends up obtaining the release of about twenty people. Other cases will be examined the next day. Sadrin returns home satisfied.

But Vigier has not yet ended his evening. He must now give an account of how the situation has evolved to Bout de l'An. And it is here that things take a turn for the worse. Upon hearing Vigier's decisions, Bout de l'An is furious: not only is his wife still missing, but the prisoners are being released for nothing in return! Things will not happen that way: just because he is small in stature does not mean that he is not a tough man. Bout de l'An then makes a triple decision. First of all, he orders Vigier to recapture all the prisoners that he has just released and send them to him in Vichy. Second, he composes an ultimatum: if his wife is not set free in the next forty-eight hours, he will execute the prisoners (thus transformed in turn, as of this moment, into hostages) and destroy the town entirely. Having hung up the phone, Bout de l'An dictates the text of his message so that posters announcing it may be prepared immediately and sent to Saint-Amand the next morning. Next he makes a third decision, the one with the heaviest consequences. He tells himself that Vigier is not the man for the job: too involved in local life, he is lacking in steadiness. Bout de l'An then remembers a firm-handed man who just happens to be free at this time, and he has him brought in. The man in question is Joseph Lécussan.

Lécussan is one of the heavyweights of the militia, literally as well as figuratively speaking. A redhead approaching his fifties, one meter eighty-three centimeters tall, corpulent, and strong, he is a former naval officer, a *cagoulard*,[22] a man of action. A man of convictions as well, he is a frenetic anticommunist (his idol is Franco) and, especially, a virulent anti-Semite, which earned him his first important appointment under Vichy: he became director of Jewish affairs in Toulouse. He quickly achieved celebrity through the systematic harassment he inflicted on the Jews as well as the extortion of money he regularly practiced. "In tribute to him, the anti-Semitic medical students at the University of Toulouse offer him a star of David made from human skin, cut from the corpse of a Jew. Lécussan will keep this delicate present for years. From time to time, he shows it off and says, 'This is from the buttocks!'" (Delperrié, 1:179)

Lécussan joined the militia in March 1943. Shortly thereafter he became its regional head in Lyons (Touvier worked for Lécussan, but their relations were not always good). Among other, more routine actions, two stand out: in November 1943, in Annecy, he personally executed an elderly Jew, Elie Dreyfus, in retaliation for the murder of a militiaman by the FTP; in January 1944 he killed with his own hands Victor Basch, age eighty, president of the League of the Rights of Man and also a Jew. Finally, it was decided within the upper administration of the militia that Lécussan's extortions of money were going too far; Bout de l'An investigated him and fired him in April. He was detained for a few weeks, then

22. *Cagoulards* were members of the Cagoule, a secret organization on the extreme right in France in the 1930s that carried out bombings, political assassinations, and other acts of terrorism, primarily in the Paris region. Several leaders of the organization later went on to occupy important positions at Vichy.

released, and since then has remained without work. It is at this time that Bout de l'An remembers him and has him appointed at Saint-Amand.

Lécussan is an arrogant but not uncultivated person. He likes to "philosophize," on the theme, for example, of why the Jews constitute a threat to the world. He is equally known for his irritable character, especially when he has been drinking. In fact, he is an alcoholic, which, it must be noted, is after all a choice and therefore in no way represents an extenuating circumstance. Such is the individual who will have the duty of repairing the damage suffered on June 6 and 7 by the militia of Saint-Amand.

A C T 2

NEGOTIATIONS

The Deal

The next morning, June 10, the posters arrive from Vichy. They give the maquisards two days, until Monday morning, June 12, at 10:00 A.M., to turn over Simone Bout de l'An; after that time, retaliation will begin. At this juncture, Sadrin returns to the subprefecture. He has retained his optimistic impressions from the night before. Once in Vigier's office, he asks him to please release the remaining hostages. It is thus a rude awakening when he hears Vigier's refusal and learns of Bout de l'An's ultimatum. He is crushed: his town will be destroyed, and his citizens will be subjected to unbridled violence.

Then he begins to think very quickly. If the situation is particularly appalling, it is because the maquisards are not even aware of the demand addressed to them. Thus, they must be found in short order and persuaded to release their precious hostage. As for Bout de l'An, surely he would prefer to get his wife back rather than massacre sixty people he does not even know. If it were possible to put the two parties in contact with each other, the outcome could be double satisfaction instead of a double massacre: the families of Resistance members would return home safe and sound, and Simone would too. What is missing is someone who can act as a mediator between the two enemy camps—and Sadrin knows where to find this person.

He therefore proposes a deal to Vigier: I give you Bout de l'An's wife; you give me my hostages and spare my town. Surprised, Vigier hesitates for a minute. He now knows from experience that the boss does not find all of his initiatives to be felicitous but thinks nevertheless that he can accept this proposal. In so doing he will have the best of both worlds: good local relations (by avoiding retaliation) and the good graces of his boss (by finding his wife), all without going to too much trouble. He thus gives his consent to Sadrin and promises to help him. For his part, Sadrin asks that in the meantime the hostages not be mistreated and that they be left where they are.

Sadrin has taken a clear risk by making this proposal, but he does not hesitate for an instant. As he writes on this very day in his appeal addressed to the population, the best that can be done at such a moment is not to pretend one has always been right or to nurse one's pride but rather to get everything under way to "relieve the pitiful sufferings" that strike one's fellow citizens (Delalande, 25). Yet the fact remains that he has no idea of where to find Bout de l'An's wife. The first step will thus be to put out a call for information. He composes a proclamation addressed "to the Saint-Amand population," summoning it to give him all the information it has at its disposal, and a communiqué for the radio, destined to the "leaders of the Resistance movement," insistently asking them to get in touch with him.

Sadrin also decides not to act alone and calls on the representative of the administration, the ephemeral replacement for the subprefect, François Villatte, whom he trusts and esteems. The two men agree to meet at 2:00 P.M. in front of the subprefecture. Sadrin must still take care of having his proclamation printed up and writing messages for the mayors of neighboring towns. Resigned, he notes in his memoirs, "It was written that on that day I would go without eating lunch" (p. 203). Half of the first day allotted by the ultimatum has already passed. At 2:00 P.M. he is front of the subprefecture, where he meets Villatte, who is accompanied by a man who sits behind the wheel of an old Rosengart, a three-seated limousine, with two pieces of white sheet hanging from the windows. It is Captain Delalande.

Delalande is an officer in the colonial infantry who has been in Indochina and the Ivory Coast. After his demobilization he worked for the AS and took refuge in Saint-Amand—a quiet little spot!—where he is employed at the subprefecture in charge of Franco-German relations (he speaks German). He has kept some contacts with the Resistance but not with its local leaders. Delalande has an enterprising and adventurous character and is in addition a master behind the wheel. It is therefore only logical that, late in the morning, Villatte (whose character is more level-headed and prudent) calls on him to accompany the mediators on their search for the maquisards, asking him to do all he can to get a car. Delalande then remembers a doctor's car, succeeds in getting hold of it, finds some gas, and manages, with some effort, to get it going. His wife has sewn two pieces of white sheet for it which, in these troubled times, are supposed to signal the peaceful intentions of the car's occupants.

It is 3:00 P.M. The search can begin.

In Search of the Maquis

Sadrin has received the same information that Bout de l'An had the night before: the trip to Maupioux by Simone and the militiamen has not gone unnoticed. The Rosengart thus heads out, at forty kilometers per hour, on the sunny roads of the Berry. They first pass through Clairins, since it is there that everyone initially met to launch the insurrection on June 6, and they then head toward the forest warden's house in the forest of Meillant, north of Saint-Amand. The car travels through several villages but stirs no enthusiasm in the inhabitants. In spite of its white cloths floating in the air—one hung under the hood of the car, the other on the door—the streets become empty as it passes. The militiamen's run through the town from the night before has left a bad taste in everyone's mouth. The surrounding countryside keeps its secrets well; the *bouchures*, or hedges separating the fields, that are found everywhere, prevent one from seeing far off. Sadrin and his companions turn into the forest; "no one looking like a maquisard appears" (Delalande, 34). They arrive in Maupioux. The forest warden, still traumatized by the shooting of the night before, tells them all about it but can give no information concerning the present location of Simone Bout de l'An. Disappointed, the negotiators leave for Saint-Amand once again. They ask questions of the people they meet along the way: still nothing. They return to town at about 7:00 P.M., and the streets are deserted, the curfew being set at 6:00 P.M. The first day of the ultimatum has passed, to no avail.

Sadrin learns that Bout de l'An telephoned in the afternoon to confirm his threats. He goes back home and gets into bed, but at 2:00 in the morning (it is now June 11), there is a knock at the door: two policemen ask him to accompany them to the subprefecture, where the head militiamen wish to speak to him. Sadrin gets dressed and accompanies them there. Here is what he discovers: during the afternoon and in the evening, Vigier put into operation the directives from Vichy. He has ordered the reconstitution of the whole group of hostages. It was necessary to retake certain ones from among those let go the night before; but most important, he wanted to arrest those close to the maquisards who kidnapped Simone. The mother of one Resistance fighter recounts:

At 1:00 in the morning, there is the pounding of a rifle butt on my door.

"Is your son there?"

"I don't know."

"Get dressed and follow us."

I followed them, their gun was touching me in the back, as if I were a criminal. My daughter shouted, "Don't stay for long, Mama, come back!"

The militiamen know on which doors to knock, but their information is not complete; for example, Blanchard's mother-in-law, who just got home from the burial of her son-in-law, Sagnelonge, is arrested, not because her two daughters have married maquisards but for having sold her café to Van Gaver in 1942. In all, sixty-five prisoners are crammed into the offices of the sub-prefecture.

Moreover, Bout de l'An's special envoy, responsible for taking over the hostage affair, arrived during the evening. When Sadrin pushes open the door to the subprefect's office at 2:30 A.M., he first sees twenty or so people seated along the walls—the extra hostages—and then, behind the subprefect's desk, Joseph Lécussan, all strapped up tight in his uniform. Instead of useless papers, lined up on the desk are a large revolver, some hand grenades, and several half-empty bottles of good vintage wine. When the introductions are over, Lécussan declares that the prisoners are guilty of the disturbances of June 6 and 7 and announces his intention to have the hostages executed if Simone is not returned within the specified time. Without hesitating, Sadrin protests: "I guarantee you that not one of these persons present is guilty of those misdeeds. If you must have a hostage, take me, shoot me, but let these innocent people go!" Lécussan rejects the proposal with a wave of his hand; such an arrangement does not suit him. He maintains his decision; he will take the hostages to Vichy first thing in the morning. "And what about the mission of mediation that Vigier gave me?" (Sadrin, 210). A little embarrassed, Vigier confirms its existence. Lécussan cares nothing about it. Sadrin withdraws; he only has one day to find the maquis. Taking advantage of the brouhaha, two prisoners manage to escape the vigilance of the militiamen and slip outdoors.

The appeal to the population brings some results. A certain Riche proposes to enter into contact with the resisters; the mayor encourages him, and he leaves by bicycle. With this semblance of good news, Sadrin returns to see Vigier and asks him to push back the ultimatum. Vigier, free of Lécussan, who has gone to Vichy with the hostages, telephones Bout de l'An and gets an extra twenty-four hours; the negotiators now have the day of Monday, June 12, at their disposal. At the same time, Vigier transmits to the mayor a piece of information that he has just received: the maquisards are said to be holding Simone in a château in the area around Urçay in the nearby Allier region; and Vigier, leading his militiamen, proposes to take the château by assault. Sadrin remains skeptical but does not want to neglect any lead, so the three negotiators are in the car as of 8:00 in the morning.

The weather is still beautiful, the rivers meander peacefully, and the countryside is romantic, but the roads are deserted and the village streets empty as the limousine approaches, still decorated with its white flags. The rare peasants they encounter have seen no one and know nothing. First château: a distinguished owner, a magnificent sitting room, period furniture but not the slightest trace of any resisters. Second château: a "charming maid" (Delalande, 45) opens the door; there is modern furniture, and refreshments are served, but still nothing. The lead appears decidedly bad, and it is almost lunchtime, so they go back to Saint-Amand.

In the afternoon the team departs again, this time in the direction of Saulzais-le-Potier, a village whose mayor is known for his Resistance sympathies. In spite of the fright caused by the pieces of white sheet, the mayor comes to meet with the negotiators. They drink a glass of wine from his vineyard. He knows nothing but suggests they push on to Châteaumeillant. It is getting late, though, so they have to put off the trip until the next morning. However, scarcely have they returned home when they receive a new message: they are to meet with the Resistance at 2:00 in the morning, on the road to the south of Châteaumeillant. In the meantime the radio has transmitted a message intended for the maquisards from Bout de l'An, who proposes to exchange the hostages in Vichy for all the women held (not just Simone); there is no mention of the men.

At 9:00 P.M. the negotiators leave again, for the third time that day. They stop at the agreed upon place, four kilometers from Châteaumeillant. It is too early, so Sadrin and Villatte doze in the car while Delalande crouches in a ditch and watches for the maquisards. A car goes by at about 11:00, but it is still not time, and the negotiators stay hidden. The hours pass, one after another. The humidity sinks down on them, the cold is beginning to get to the men on the lookout. Two o'clock in the morning, nothing; three o'clock, still nothing. Disappointed, they decide to leave (actually, the maquisards of Châteaumeillant are waiting for them but on another road; there was a misunderstanding). The car has gotten cold and refuses to start. They have to push it a hundred meters or so before it will start and then get in. They manage to do it, but Sadrin, who is not as young as he used to be, sprains his ankle while jumping. It is raining, the windshield wiper does not work, and the headlights barely light up the road.

They get back home, exhausted and frustrated, at 5:00 in the morning.

The Hostages in Vichy

On the morning of June 11, Lécussan and a few other militiamen have fifty-six hostages board some buses and then leave with them. Seven or eight hostages remain locked up on the third floor of the post office, which is temporarily transformed into a prison. All those detained have had a bad night. The militiamen, who know by now that they can do with them as they please, amuse themselves by scaring them. Le Lanchon has gathered the women and juggles a grenade in front of them, asking, "Do you want to explode now?" Then he takes his machine gun and points it at one of them: "Should I start with you?" Some get hysterical. Most of the hostages belong to the families of the resisters, but there are also a few persons presumed to be directly responsible for the insurrection, such as Colonel Larouquette and the pharmacist, Théogène Chavaillon, who is said to have been walking about town with a hunting rifle on June 7. More simply, there are some who had the misfortune of not pleasing one of the militiamen. On this same morning, the militiamen who have stayed in town try to blow up a few buildings, deemed guilty by association with the Resistance fighters: the Rex movie house, once again, and the café du Théâtre (because the two sons of the owners have gone off to the maquis). But the buildings remain standing.

The convoy sets off in the direction of Vichy. The buses are accompanied by armored cars and motorbikes. They avoid the forest of Tronçais to eliminate the risk of meeting maquisards. At noon they are in Vichy, and everyone gets off at the race track, in front of the wooden sheds set up there. Francis Bout de l'An is there, accompanied by his mother and several members of his administrative staff. He makes a speech to the hostages: if, on the next day, June 12, before 10:00 in the morning, Simone and the other women have not been let go, the hostages will be executed in groups of ten—first the men, then the women. Then the town of Saint-Amand, where the hostages left their families, will be razed by bombs and burned down. This speech reveals a Bout de l'An who is out of control and who seeks to avenge himself for the humiliation he has endured by delighting in his superiority over the prisoners and by inflicting moral torture on them. In their position they obviously cannot do a thing to speed up Simone's release.

Then comes the time for interrogations and physical torture. They begin with the men, and the women are obliged to be present at the spectacle. In the presence of Darnand, who has made the trip for the occasion, Bout de l'An himself and his helpers attack these shackled men and beat them black and blue. It is Tahar Kador who receives the most blows. He was said to have been seen carrying a weapon, but besides this, he has the added fault of being Algerian. When the session is over, blood is everywhere, and he is unrecognizable. A policeman suspected of conspiring with the terrorists is also severely beaten. Darnand is surprised and asks, "Why are you waiting to shoot him?" The other men are also beaten. When night has fallen, the women are led into the buildings, and for the men, mock executions begin. Bout de l'An takes thirty-two of them and divides them up into groups of eight; then he makes a first group line up in front of the barn, facing the machine guns. Then he changes his mind and has them replaced by the next eight. Next he orders them to lie down in the mud, to get back up, and to lie down again. At 1:00 in the morning, a tired Bout de l'An goes home, and the hostages are locked up for the night in the sheds.

The militiamen also interrogate the women (an interrogation with no other purpose but to intimidate). Thérèse Lamoureux, age sixteen, is among the women, and instead of keeping in the background, she tells the militiamen that she prefers the maquisards to them. Whips and clubs are brought in. She is asked where the Resistance has gone, meaning her father and brother, but she does not answer.

"You are going to tell the truth or you will be undressed immediately."

"Go ahead, I'm built like any other woman." Exasperated, the militiamen leave her for a minute. At 10:00 P.M., Bout de l'An interrogates her himself.

"We could use some feisty girls like you in the militia," he says before threatening her. "It's a shame to die so young."

"Now is as good a time as later," replies Thérèse, unfazed.

The next day, Lécussan will come to interrogate her, vaunting the merits of the militiamen and their German friends. Thérèse maintains her insolent attitude (Delalande, 137–38). The women are not beaten.

The next morning, June 12, the time limit theoretically expires at 10:00. But shortly before then the hostages are told that it has been extended until that evening, for contacts with the maquis have been established (through Riche's trip). Then the men are again separated from the women, with the exception of two or three who are sick and are taken to the château des Brosses, an opulent home on the road to Charmeil, a political prison and torture center for the militia. The two groups are thus locked up separately to wait for negotiations to progress.

The Surcouf in the Creuse

At Bosmoreau-les-Mines, the day of June 10 is devoted to rest, much needed after the several tumultuous days and nights preceding it, and to dividing the Cher group into two smaller units. Lalonnier's second in command goes from one person to another and asks each one if he is coming with the FTP or staying with Combat. To most of the maquisards, these acronyms are meaningless, for they just joined the Resistance on June 6 or 7 and are there to fight the Krauts and liberate France, not to get involved in politics. So the question really is whether each one is going with Hubert (Lalonnier) or with Surcouf (Blanchard) — Van Gaver is out of the picture right now; the military men are calling the shots, not the politicians. The division is made primarily along the lines of friendships and acquaintanceships, but it nonetheless corresponds to the split between Combat and FTP. The fusion of the two networks is too recent to override former affiliations. But this does not mean that the groups are politically homogeneous. There are apolitical members among the FTP, and in Combat the range of political opinions is particularly wide since it includes Communists as well as some former members of Action française.[23]

23. Action française was an extreme right wing nationalist and monarchist movement founded in 1908 and directed by Charles Maurras, a writer and ideologue. His influence on the Vichy regime was extensive, and his work was censored following the Liberation.

Each of the newly constituted groups has about 150 people. Arms are also divided up, but not half and half. Since they belonged primarily to Combat before, Blanchard keeps most of them, even though he does let the FTP have some of them.

On this particular day, Radio London is transmitting a new message from General Koenig, supreme commander of the FFI: "Given the present impossibility of resupplying provisions, weapons and ammunition, desist as much as possible, I repeat, desist as much as possible from guerrilla activity, form small, isolated groups rather than large detachments" (Kriegel-Valrimont, 40). Do Van Gaver and Blanchard receive this message that would seem to indicate that they were wrong to stage the insurrection on June 6? In any case, it recommends the formation of small groups, and that is precisely what they are doing.

On June 11 everything is ready for the departure. The Blanchard group, which now takes the battle name of its leader and is called the Surcouf Company, will go a few kilometers south and occupy the château de Mérignat and the adjoining farms. They take with them the prisoners, with whom Lalonnier cannot be bothered anyway. He himself will lead his men a few kilometers north, into the area around Janaillat.

Before they leave, however, there is a surprise: a message arrives from Saint-Amand. It is from Riche, the mayor's envoy, who left at 5:00 in the morning. He has covered more than one hundred kilometers and has reached Sainte-Feyre, south of Guéret; from there a second messenger brings Sadrin's letter to Bosmoreau-les-Mines, thirty kilometers farther south. It is Sochet who receives it, so he is the first to learn of the new situation: the departure of the hostages and Sadrin's request to enter into contact with the maquisards. Sochet quickly consults Blanchard and Van Gaver, and they agree on what course to follow. They let Riche know that he can return home and announce that a messenger will leave for Saint-Amand as soon as possible. Sochet then goes to see Simone Bout de l'An and asks her to write the following letter.

My Dear Francis,

I am in the hands of the Liberation Army. I am being treated well. Spare the hostages to avoid the worst. I have faith in God. I'm worried about the fate of the children, give them a kiss for me.

Tenderly yours,
Simone
(Delalande, 62)

We have come full circle. Simone now appears as a hostage who ensures the safety of the hostages from Saint-Amand, who themselves ensure the safety of Simone. They reflect identical images back and forth to each other; they imitate one another. Indeed, if the resisters were initially able to think they needed to take hostages to keep the town from being subject to retaliation in response to their takeover of it, the situation now has been changed: German repression is over, the storm has passed, and the dangers that presently threaten the town are a direct result of the taking of hostages, which was intended to prevent retaliation. Basically, as of this moment the militiamen and the maquisards should be able to reach an understanding, for their goals coincide: release the hostages, on both sides. But their agreement on the final objective is not enough to begin a transaction; reaching an understanding requires that a climate of mutual trust first be established, for only that trust will make negotiations possible. For the moment, though, there is no trace of it.

With the letter in hand, Fernand Sochet now gets on a bicycle and leaves for the region of the Cher. Sadrin has been asking for the cooperation of the mayors of neighboring towns, and Sochet will take his missive not to Saint-Amand itself, which would be too dangerous, but to the mayor of a town in the area. The task turns out to be more difficult than imagined, however. Sochet goes from one village to another, and no mayor is willing to accept the letter, which is thought to be too explosive. Each one figures that it is no time to advertise that the Resistance has faith in him. Finally, late at night, the secretary at the mayor's office in

Saint-Baudel, a locality northwest of Saint-Amand, courageously accepts the letter.

In the meantime those who are temporarily occupying the village of Bosmoreau-les-Mines have left. In the afternoon of the same day, June 11, the FTP has an encounter with some German armed detachments and succeeds in extricating itself. A few days later the FTP goes into its permanent quarters a little to the east, in the vicinity of Sardent, preserving its autonomy in relation to the FFI of "François." Each platoon, composed of about twenty-five men, is moved in separately. A repentant militiaman and a German prisoner are responsible for doing the cooking. In the month that follows, until mid-July, they are engaged in the usual activities of maquisards. They also make a nocturnal raid on other resisters to steal some weapons; Lalonnier has never been one to let bourgeois legality stand in his way.

The château de Mérignat and its outbuildings form a hamlet in the middle of an undulating green countryside. There is even a little chapel there, although it is closed. The Surcouf settles in comfortably. The leaders (Blanchard, Van Gaver, Le Quellec, Chaillaud, and five or six others) stay in the master's house. The trucks are camouflaged under the trees, and the group of drivers sleeps beside them. Each platoon—there are five of them—moves into one of the barns of the adjoining farms.

Daily life is organized, little by little. In the days that follow, the Surcouf receives parachute drops of arms, provisions (Blanchard even sends tobacco to Lalonnier), and money. They are thus able to pay for the goods they need. One of the maquisards recalls, "I never ate as much meat in my life. We had a butcher with us, and he killed a calf every day. But the menu was monotonous: at noon and in the evening, veal stew with potatoes, always the same old thing."

On certain days, though, crêpes are served. They have no coffee, but they find some chocolate, so every morning they drink hot chocolate with milk. On several occasions a messenger goes to

Saint-Amand to deliver news to the families of the Resistance fighters. Blanchard has left behind there not only his young wife but also a little girl several months old, and Van Gaver has two children; as husbands and fathers, they are worried.

Blanchard carefully watches out so that no one "requisitions" anything for personal use. One maquisard helps himself in a tobacco shop, promising to pay after the Liberation. Blanchard gets wind of the incident, takes the guilty party back to the scene, and makes him pay up and apologize. Another day a silver tray disappears from the dishware of the château. Blanchard gathers his men and warns them: "If the tray is not returned during the night, I'm turning the matter over to François." "François" is their superior officer (since they are in the Creuse) and has a fearsome reputation. It is said that he did not hesitate to have one of his men executed because he did not behave as he should have during an attack: "I have no need of men who are scared to death." The next morning the tray is back where it belongs.

Actual resistance activities essentially consist of learning how to handle weapons better, something of which the new recruits have only a faint idea. They do not lack ammunition, but first of all, it is not always the right kind (the company has two machine guns dating from World War I), and second, silence is recommended so that the Germans will not be able to discover their location. Nevertheless, each man now has a weapon, 150 bullets around his waist, and two grenades hanging from his belt. The men go to parachute drops approximately once every three nights. They also monitor the roads, set up ambushes, and fire at military targets that seem vulnerable. The rest of the time they walk around and play cards.

The prisoners are put in the chapel, the men on the left and the women on the right of a makeshift partition. They are made to take a walk every day. They are now guarded by those called "veterans," or even "grandfathers": men in their forties who are judged unsuited for dangerous military actions. Certain maquisards remember crossing paths with Simone Bout de l'An and speaking to her. A sort of mutual respect is established but not one that goes as far as constituting agreement. Simone does not disavow her own people; she repeats that the militiamen are also struggling for the liberation of France, even if it is not in the same manner as that of the maquisards. But for the majority of the company, the militiamen have become invisible, and they think about them less and less.

First Contacts

On the morning of June 12, only a few hours after their nocturnal expedition to Châteaumeillant, the negotiators regain some hope. Although the ultimatum expires that evening, they have received two encouraging pieces of news, both of which are the consequence of Riche's heroic bicycle trip in the Creuse. The first piece of news comes from Riche himself, who is set to meet the mayor that very morning. The mayor, in turn, gets on a bike (he discovers that his sprained ankle does not prevent him from pedaling) and travels to an isolated farm in the area around Saint-Amand. There he finds Riche, exhausted from his trip the previous night but happy at having accomplished his mission: he has transmitted the mayor's letter to one of the Resistance leaders, and he knows that he will have the answer too. Sadrin then proposes to Riche that he take his place on the negotiating team because Sadrin's new infirmity requires him to stay in town.

It is also in the morning that another event takes place: the mayor of Saint-Baudel telephones the subprefecture to announce the presence of the letter from Simone. The militiamen are fearful that it is a trap. As a result, the untiring Delalande and the persistent Villatte take on the job of going to get it. They travel to Saint-Baudel and retrieve the sealed letter. They hurry along, but a herd of cows on the road slows them down, and when they arrive back at the subprefecture, it is already 3:00 P.M. Vigier reads the letter, informs them of its contents, and immediately calls Bout de l'An. At first, Bout de l'An is skeptical. "Liberation army," "treated well"—it all sounds like dictation from a maquisard. What if his wife was executed right after she wrote those words? But Vigier rereads the letter to him, and he realizes that several expressions come straight from Simone. Despite the contrary opinion of Lécussan, who is at his side and who sees in all this only stall tactics on the part of the maquis ("I've had it up to here with them!"), he agrees to extend the ultimatum by forty-eight hours. The negotiators now have until the evening of June 14 to find his wife.

The new team—Delalande, Villatte, Riche—meets in the late afternoon. They are convinced that the resisters are acting in good faith and that Simone is alive, but where are they? Unfortunately, the letter gives no indication concerning the next stage of negotiation. Without more specifics the three men cannot simply go "into the Creuse" to look for their interlocutors; they need an intermediary to lead them. They leave again for Châteaumeillant. Perhaps the missed rendezvous was for tonight? The village streets continue to clear out when they arrive, in spite of the pieces of white sheet signifying peace that hang from their Rosengart. There is a new wait on the road to Châteaumeillant and a new disappointment. They spend the rest of the night in the little town. On the morning of June 13 they are informed of a new meeting with local Resistance officials at 1:00 in the afternoon, and go to it.

The meeting takes place on a path in the middle of the vineyards. Five maquisards from the Châteaumeillant area step forth, the same ones who waited on another road the night before. The atmosphere is relaxed, but these maquisards do not really know very much. Is Bout de l'An's wife still alive? Surely. Has she been mistreated? It's not very likely. One of the maquisards, the teacher named Mignaton, adds: "We find it ridiculous to attack women. If we had Bout de l'An's wife, we would give her back immediately, but we're not the ones holding her" (Delalande, 78). So then who has her? The maquis of Saint-Amand. How does one get together with them? A volunteer steps forth, Roger Jarrige. He is from Saint-Amand; he took part in the occupation of the town, went into the Creuse, and is now back in the area. He knows the maquisards' hiding places and is willing to carry a new message to them.

On the next morning, June 14, Delalande and Villatte leave again, this time in a new, faster car loaned by the militia. They find Jarrige, who, in turn, borrows the car and goes off into the Creuse, where he is expected at 2:00. Delalande and Villatte resign themselves to waiting in the next village, at the mayor's house. A little wine to whet the appetite, "a country-style meal that would have been the envy of all Paris," "a cup of roast barley coffee, a small glass of brandy," and they are ready to go again (Delalande, 95). We are well informed about the meals eaten during this period, thanks to the memoirs written shortly afterward. Since food has become a problem for people in the towns, each good meal makes an impression on them. It must be said that in the countryside of Saint-Amand, people live no worse during the war than before; on the contrary, the prices for farm products have climbed, and farmers actually make more money.

Evening falls, but Jarrige does not return. The negotiators decide to spend the night where they are. They try to telephone Saint-Amand to explain their delay (the ultimatum expires that very evening), but the line is cut. They do not sleep very well. The next morning, June 15 (copious breakfast, cold cuts of pork and milk products), Jarrige is finally there. He recounts that the night before, he met with "Roger," one of the lieutenants of "François," and asked for his help. Unfortunately, "Roger" does not know how to or does not want to contact the leaders of the Surcouf. He therefore decides to turn the matter over to his superior, "François." This allows him to play a more important role himself. The initial reaction of "François," recounted to Jarrige by "Roger," is clearly negative. He is said to have declared, for the benefit of the negotiators: "Tell them to get lost if they don't want to have to deal with me. Bout de l'An's wife is just fine where she is, and we are going to keep her. Nothing will change that, whatever happens" (Delalande, 105).

The negotiators are dismayed. They have come so close to their goal only to see their efforts fail. There remains for them only a glimmer of hope: "Roger" has suggested that they personally meet with "François" to try to change his mind. Still, they decide to hide the bad news, indeed to disguise it as good news, by telling the militiamen only about having made contact. So at midday they return home to Saint-Amand.

Having remained in town since June 12, Sadrin consults on June 13 with five local officials, representatives of the legal system, the church, the army, and social services. He proposes that they step forward with him as hostages in place of the imprisoned families (he may be thinking of the burghers of Calais).[24] The proposal is transmitted to Vichy, but Bout de l'An takes no action on it. On the other hand, he calls the mayor at 5:00 P.M. to ask him for news of his wife. Upon hearing that there is still nothing specific, he reiterates his threats should the terrorists not come forward before the next night. He adds: "Even if I have to be called Bout de l'An the Butcher for it, the hostages will be executed and the town will be completely destroyed" (Sadrin, 222). Does he seriously think this, or is he trying to reinforce his image as the implacable leader?

In any case, Sadrin takes the threats seriously and is alarmed. He then remembers the proposal, one Dr. Roques made to him, to step in and speak to the archbishop of Bourges, and calls him. Dr. Roques leaves right away and at 8:30 arrives at the archdiocese, interrupting the prelate's dinner. The archbishop immediately sees him and takes the matter seriously. On the morning of June 14 he

24. During the Hundred Years War the town of Calais was saved from destruction by the courage of six town notables who presented themselves as hostages to the British king. A celebrated sculpture by Rodin commemorates the event.

is led by Dr. Roques to Saint-Amand and finds Vigier and Sadrin at the subprefecture. He pleads the case for the hostages, but Vigier does not want to hear a word of it; besides, nothing depends on him. Still accompanied by Dr. Roques, Msgr. Lefebvre goes on his way to Vichy, where he is received by Bout de l'An in the afternoon. He first asks for leniency in the name of Christian charity and of justice (why punish those who have done nothing?). Bout de l'An turns a deaf ear. Then, as the mayor did, the archbishop proposes himself to take the place of the hostages. This offer is also rejected. He then resorts to the language of reason: if Bout de l'An maintains his decision and executes the hostages, as he says he will this evening, he can be sure that he will never again see his wife alive, and his children will never see their mother again. This time the argument carries. Bout de l'An decides to suspend his threats—without canceling them, however—as long as there is some hope of seeing his wife return and thus as long as negotiations go on. Starting at this moment, the hostages will no longer be beaten, and three of them, who from all indications were arrested by mistake, will even be set free and sent back to Saint-Amand.

Left to himself, Sadrin writes a petition to Laval; he will never receive an answer. The next day, June 15, at the usual 3:00 P.M. time, there is a new call from Bout de l'An. Having given up ruthless punishment for the time being, he nevertheless tries to maintain pressure on the town. He announces to Sadrin that if negotiations should fail, he will deprive the town of gas, electricity, and water; children will no longer have milk. Only the hospital will be exempt from these measures, for Bout de l'An's children were cared for there. Sadrin protests: why blame the town for what happened? It was up to the militiamen to keep his wife safe. He then discovers that the militiamen are no more highly esteemed in their leader's eyes than are the other inhabitants of the town: "The militiamen? I don't give a damn about them. They should have fought to the death defending the woman they were supposed to protect" (Sadrin, 224).

In fact, Bout de l'An will never seek to obtain the release of the militiamen. Their lives do not count for him.

With the Head of the Militia

After returning to Saint-Amand, Villatte is discouraged; he has the impression that they will not get anything. Delalande, more optimistic by nature, wants to continue to try everything. Although he was recruited only as a chauffeur in the beginning, his personal qualities, his spirit of initiative, and his tenacity make him at this moment the top negotiator, the chief mediator.

The two men go to Vigier's and try to present the way the matter has evolved in a favorable light. They will go to meet with chief leader "François," and they will obtain Simone's release. But what exactly are the terms of the exchange? No one knows. Vigier suggests that it would be best to go and ask the question of Bout de l'An himself. The negotiators regain some hope; they are ready to leave immediately.

At 5:00 P.M., they get into Vigier's car, escorted by other militiamen. They make a stop at Sancoins, where Vigier introduces them to his family, and then they continue on toward Vichy. All the barricades that the German army has set up on the road are opened at the words "French militia." At 7:00 the cars stop in front of the Modern Hotel, seat of the militia. Vigier leads Delalande and Villatte into a small office decorated with a portrait of Darnand. Francis Bout de l'An appears.

Delalande (115–29) has recounted in detail this first meeting with the assistant secretary-general of the militia. Bout de l'An is surrounded by his staff, Lécussan is also present, and they all smoke "cigarette after cigarette or pipe after pipe." The terms of the exchange are specified without too much difficulty: the maquis must set free all the women it is holding prisoner (Bout de l'An confirms his lack of interest in the fate of the men: "they are soldiers; they should have fought"), and he, for his part, will release all those among the Vichy hostages who were arrested unarmed, including the pharmacist Chavaillon, whose hunting rifle is not considered a serious threat. On the other hand, he refuses to make any political gesture whatsoever to facilitate the release of his family: "Even if they were to threaten my wife with death in order to put pressure on me, I wouldn't change my politics in the slightest." He obviously fears opening himself up to a spiral of blackmail that could go on for who knows how long, but it is also apparent that he is an "idealist," that is, someone who prefers principles to human beings. It looks as though Bout de l'An is anxious to get his wife back more out of pride than out of love, that he would rather lose his wife than lose face.

And what if the women, in particular his wife, were not released, or if they were executed? For Bout de l'An assumes—and rightly so—that the "letter was written under duress" and fears that his wife has since been killed. It is equally possible that the maquisards will simply refuse negotiation. If events take that particular turn, Bout de l'An will have recourse to several forms of retaliation that, in truth, are not very consistent with each other. The negotiators nevertheless take these threats seriously. The massacre of Oradour-sur-Glane in the Limousin region (nearly a thousand dead, executed by the SS as retaliation)[25] is still fresh; it goes back only to June 10. Bout de l'An will starve the town and then burn it down with bombs. He will turn the investigation over to the German armed forces, who will conduct it with their well-known brutality. He will have all the hostages shot to death after he has brought them before the court (and clearly, no matter what the

25. About two o'clock on the afternoon of June 10, 1944, some 120 German troops of the SS Das Reich Division arrived in the village of Oradour-sur-Glane and rounded up the men, women, and children. The women and children were taken to the village church, which was then set on fire. The men were gunned down by machine gun fire. Only a few individuals survived. The massacre at Oradour was supposedly undertaken as an act of reprisal for Resistance operations against the Germans in the region. For a detailed account of the incident and the role Oradour has played in the French memory of the war, see Sara Farmer, *Oradour: Arrêt sur mémoire* (Paris: Calmann Lévy, 1994).

verdict). He will arrest the wives of all the leaders of the maquis or other rebellious sorts, and he will have their property seized. In short, he will answer every blow, but he will do it by going one step further.

"It's the law of an eye for an eye!" exclaims Delalande.

"It's up to the terrorists to humanize our disagreement," retorts Bout de l'An. There is, however, little chance that anyone will take the first step in the direction of humanity, since in this exchange the appeal to justice is perceived as a sign of weakness, and here it is a matter of a test of strength.

These talks go hand in hand with a background discussion. Bout de l'An never forgets his "principles." For one thing, in the context of nationalistic overstatement he refuses to acknowledge his guilt for collaborating with the Germans: "The terrorists receive lots of arms and money from the British." For another thing, his fight is ideologically just: he is struggling against communism, which must be hunted down throughout Europe. As foreigners go, the Germans are preferable to the British because the British are helping the Communists, whereas the Germans are fighting against them. The conclusion, justifying his overall commitment and that of the militia: the terrorists, individuals with no faith or law, "are people to be exterminated, if France is ever to recover." Here Bout de l'An echoes the words of the FTP chiefs, words that are also those of all totalitarians: the enemies are not even human, the purification of the collective soul requires the elimination of all that is foreign to it, the death of the scapegoat must assure the survival of the community.

Once the talks are over, Bout de l'An invites the negotiators to dinner. The meal, served in a restaurant, is "delicious, with plenty of wine" (Delalande, 133). Delalande suddenly gets an idea: perhaps they could visit the hostages from Saint-Amand detained in Vichy? Lécussan then takes his pipe out of his mouth and steps in to oppose the idea. Humanitarian gestures can be made only on a reciprocal basis, and the negotiators have not seen the maquis' hostages. Moreover, Lécussan has great difficulty understanding Delalande's insistence because he does not see what his personal interest in this could be, and doesn't one act always and only out of one's own interest? Delalande is relentless; sharper and sharper words are exchanged. Finally, Bout de l'An intervenes and settles it. A visit is authorized but only to the women, at the race track then, not at the château des Brosses. Vigier leads them there, and they go to the sheds where about fifteen women and a few disabled men are crowded together. Words of encouragement and consolation are exchanged from both sides.

Late in the night, Delalande and Villatte return to the hôtel des Princes in Vichy. They leave again at dawn the next morning, and at 8:30 they are back in Saint-Amand.

With the Head of the Maquis

June 16: the two negotiators, this time accompanied by their guide, Jarrige, leave to complete the second part of the mission. Now that they know exactly what the conditions of the militiamen are, conditions that are reasonable after all, they have only to obtain the maquisards' assent. They go back through Châteaumeillant and Sainte-Sévère, take the bumpy back roads to avoid the dangerous main road, and arrive at Bonnat. "On a shady town square, some home distillers are making a highly rated brandy" (Delalande, 149). There Jarrige obtains authorization to go into the headquarters of "Roger," with whom he has already been in contact. They thus arrive at the Rateau farm, on the outskirts of Bonnat. "Roger" gives them a cold welcome; under the cover of a humanitarian mission, couldn't these two emissaries actually be on an espionage assignment? Besides, don't they openly work for Vigier and Bout de l'An?

Despite this, the discussion gets under way. "Roger" confirms to them that "François" is lacking in eagerness to proceed to the exchange of hostages. He claims that it is "François," not the maquis, who is holding Simone. He refuses to put them in contact with Van Gaver and Blanchard but is willing to return to see "François." Then they sit down to eat. It is a copious meal whose menu is carefully detailed by Delalande: "White bread, hors d'oeuvres, Chateaubriand with mashed potatoes, roast, cream cheese, Savoie cake, cider (for lack of wine), real coffee from a parachute drop, American cookies, brandy" (p. 158). The maquisards are well stocked. During the meal, "Roger" speaks to them of his military exploits. The others present at the meal show their approval of the temerity of their chief in the face of a much more powerful enemy.

"Roger" leaves and does not come back until late in the afternoon. "François" has agreed to meet with the negotiators the next morning at 11:00. The negotiators must therefore spend the night there. It is feared that there will be a German attack during the night. They camouflage their car and take refuge on a neighboring farm. On the morning of June 17 they have breakfast on the farm: "coffee with milk, sausage, all the bread you could want, and red wine will make up this frugal meal" (Delalande, 169). At 9:00 they depart in the direction of Sardent, to the south of Guéret, the site of the rendezvous. Shortly before they arrive there, they are stopped by a car and held at gunpoint. It is "François" and his bodyguards. The exchange thus begins on the side of the road, in the rain.

"François" is a tall man in uniform, with a Basque beret tilted over his left ear, and he is wearing tortoiseshell glasses. His brow is knit, his lips are pursed; he has a haughty attitude. Above all, he is anxious to convince his interlocutors of his legendary toughness, and he informs them that he is on the verge of arresting a dangerous female spy and has no time to lose. Already this morning he has been hard at work. He just had five of his own men executed for improper behavior. Having thus established what kind of man he is, he applies himself to putting his interlocutors where

he wants them; that is to say, to depriving them of the privilege
that would assure them a neutral position with respect to the two
parties present. No, they are not impartial mediators but rather
"messengers of the militia" (Delalande, 174). No more than Lécussan does "François" want to understand what makes them act
because he fails to see wherein their personal interest lies.

"So then, whose side are you on?"

In fact, whose side *are* they on, that of the militia or of the
maquis? Their sympathies are without doubt with the Resistance,
but they are not acting "for" it any more than they are for themselves. They are expecting no reward, and moreover, they could
remain with the maquisards and thereby escape the eventual retaliation inflicted in Saint-Amand. So why have they been travel-
ing the roads for almost ten days now, continually risking their
lives in the maquisards' ambushes and the Germans' roadblocks?
Why are there some others, like Mayor Sadrin, Archbishop Lefebvre, and the ordinary citizens Riche and Jarrige, who devote themselves to this same cause, sparing no effort? Here are a few individuals who put the dignity and lives of human beings—those of
others, not their own—above the ideals that drive the maquis and
the militia alike, hoping that their insistence will eventually make
the reigning stupidity and pride give way.

As for the exchange of hostages, to begin with, "François" does
not think it possible. To enter into interaction with someone, one
must have a minimum of trust in him, and the militiamen are
"people with no faith or law," "brutes working for the Krauts,"
scum just right for extermination. But beyond this, "François"
does not think this exchange is desirable. He does not want to free
the women, all militiawomen and spies (their crime is now having been imprisoned: they risk revealing the location of their
prison). And what does he have to gain by letting the hostages from
Saint-Amand go? "I couldn't care less about Saint-Amand, the
men needed only to go off to the maquis, as we did ourselves" (Delalande, 177). (Bout de l'An himself said that the militiamen need-

ed only to fight and they would not have been taken hostage.) "I went off," "François" continues, telling them to look at him. Then he adds, "I left a wife and two children in a safe place." (That is what Bout de l'An thought, too.) His conclusion: "We have no pity for them."

But most important, he does not want the exchange simply because it was proposed or approved of by his enemies the militiamen. If he accepted it, he would be acquiescing to their will, in other words submitting to them, showing himself as inferior. In the world of conflict everything is settled by force, and the appeal to justice or to humanity has no place in it. "If we release Bout de l'An's wife, it could be taken by the militia as a sign of weakness and of our fear of those vile traitors at the service of Germany." The important thing for "François" is not what the German authorities or the militia inflict on them as retaliation but the very fact of not giving in, of acting in accord with one's own will, not that of others. "Since you are holding to your position, I am holding to mine," he says a little later to the negotiators (Delalande, 181). To withdraw from the confrontation, from comparison with the other, is inconceivable to him. The more closely the two rivals resemble each other, the less possible it is for them to reach an understanding. "You have to understand my position as leader" — such is his explanation (which he judges to be sufficient) for his refusal to yield and to intervene to save a town of ten thousand inhabitants.

Then "François" pretends to change his mind. He remembers Subprefect Lecène, arrested June 2, and suddenly proposes to set his hostages free (he no longer fears the revelations by female spies) if, in addition to the hostages held by the militia, the German authorities agree to release Lecène. "But he was arrested by the Gestapo, not by the militia. Why bring the Germans into an exchange that they will never accept?" But for "François," Simone is an "excellent catch," and she must be traded for a high price. Militia, Gestapo — he doesn't want to get into the details of all that.

Besides, didn't Darnand join the Waffen SS? If so, he can get whatever he wants from the Gestapo. And it is a well-known fact that Simone is his mistress; he cares more about her than anything else ("François" seems to be forgetting that she was living as a recluse with her two children). Take it or leave it.

With this, "François" again leaves to take care of urgent business. The negotiators will see him again a few hours later in Sardent: the dangerous female spy is under arrest; she is in the back of his car. "François" has a drink with them but remains inflexible. The negotiators get back on the road, going home, and this time Delalande joins Villatte in his pessimism and discouragement. On his side, having returned to his command post near Vidaillat, "François" declares that he has had enough of these friends of the militiamen who claim to be mediators. If he sees them again, he will not fail to hang them. Then he tells himself that he should do something, though, about this VIP of a hostage detained by the maquis of Saint-Amand and about whom he had not concerned himself up until now. He takes his pen and writes a missive to Darnand (it is preferable to speak leader to leader rather than going through the intermediary of little people). If you touch a single hair on the heads of your hostages, he essentially tells him, your mistress, Simone Bout de l'An, will immediately be killed, cut up into pieces, and sent to you by mail.

Negotiations Stall

Exhausted from their trip and the new obstacles they have encountered, Delalande and Villatte return to Saint-Amand late in the afternoon and go directly to the subprefecture. They make their report to Vigier, who telephones Vichy. It is easy for the militiamen to underscore the maquisards' ill will. The next morning, Sunday, June 18, Msgr. Lefebvre has read in all the churches of the diocese an appeal to charity, which he addresses to both parties. Delalande goes to Sadrin's house to keep him up to date on the negotiations, or rather, their agonizing pace. He also learns that Bout de l'An continues to call the mayor's office every day at 5:00 P.M. to ask for news and to utter threats. Sadrin is so disturbed by these conversations that he decides to close the town hall fifteen minutes early—to no avail: Bout de l'An now calls the subprefecture and has his messages communicated to Sadrin.

Late in the afternoon the negotiators return to Vichy to report the demands of "François" to Bout de l'An. Bout de l'An does not want to humble himself before the Gestapo by asking for mercy for Lecène. Besides, wouldn't recommending his return to the maquis be the same as admitting his guilt (which has not yet been clearly established) before the German police, thereby making his case worse? The militia has no more confidence in the maquis than the maquis has in the militia, and there can be no transactions between them since they basically desire only one and the same thing: annihilation of the adversary.

But Bout de l'An proposes a new deal, which is in fact based on a misunderstanding. Having learned that the name of the head of the maquis is "François," he thinks he is dealing with François Valentin, against whom he holds a particularly strong grudge. Valentin had been the director of the Légion but then converted to Gaullism. Bout de l'An thus decides to arrest several wives of Resistance fighters, including Mrs. Valentin, who is said to be in labor in a Limoges clinic, in order to propose to "François" an exchange that would appear to be equitable: a spouse for a spouse. Then he adopts two complementary measures. On the one hand, having learned about the archbishop's message, he agrees to improve the conditions of captivity of his hostages. Without setting them free, he puts them under the protection of the Red Cross. Their treatment becomes less harsh indeed. But on the other hand, he decides to send Vigier back to his duties as regional head in Orléans and to replace him in Saint-Amand with Lécussan, a "stricter" man, who will be able to "put this house back in order" (Delalande, 200).

On June 19 the very weary negotiators get back on the road

home. At the subprefecture of Saint-Amand they observe with annoyance that Lécussan has already moved into the subprefect's office. He has hung on the wall behind him pictures of Darnand and Bout de l'An. He enjoins the negotiators to hurry, for these talks have gone on for too long.

On June 20 a new departure for the Creuse: after the roadblocks of the militia come those of the maquis, with identity checks and declarations of good intentions. At the Rateau farm, "Roger" is pleased to organize a new rendezvous with his leader, even if he does not think his leader will change his mind. On the return to Saint-Amand there is a new meeting with Lécussan. "This is turning out to be a real comedy, all these fruitless comings and goings," thunders Lécussan (Delalande, 209).

June 21: return to the Creuse; the rendezvous is for 11:00 A.M. in Sardent. Unfortunately, twenty kilometers short of their destination, they encounter an unforeseen obstacle: some herds of cows and sheep fill the road. The shepherd panics; Delalande honks the horn, but nothing does any good. For one kilometer the animals gallop in front of the car. Nevertheless, at 11:00 they are in Sardent, but there is no trace of "François." The hours pass; still no one. They go to the hideout of "Roger," who leads them to Pontarion and goes back off in search of "François." Finally, "François" arrives at about 5:00. After raising some objections, he ends up accepting Bout de l'An's new proposal: the Vichy hostages plus the three wives of Resistance fighters for the female hostages in the Creuse. During a slow return to Saint-Amand, Delalande dares not turn on his headlights and drives by guesswork. Without knowing it, they just miss an ambush staged by Lalonnier, whose men spotted the negotiators' car and believed its occupants to be spies working for the militia.

On June 22 Delalande and Villatte present themselves at the subprefecture where they find the personnel to be terrorized by a speech Lécussan delivered the night before. After having gathered all the employees, Lécussan laid his big revolver on the table and declared, "I am being sent here as *Gauleiter*.[26] I am firmly resolved to raze the town if asked to do so. I can have whomever I want executed, whenever I want. I demand your total submission" (Delalande, 218–19). On June 22 he modifies his vocabulary slightly: instead of *Gauleiter*, he names himself subprefect, since the job seems open (he is the fifth person to assume this function since the beginning of the month). The negotiators call Bout de l'An to announce the acceptance of his conditions, but a new disappointment awaits them: Bout de l'An tells them that he is unable to have the arrested wives go there because the railways are cut off; and as for Valentin's wife, he has not even succeeded in arresting her. Therefore, they must revert back to the preceding terms of the exchange and free hostages for hostages.

Delalande and Villatte have the rug pulled out from under them by this stroke of destiny. In addition, Lécussan presents them with a new ultimatum that only adds to their gloom. "We have had enough of the way this whole matter is dragging along. If Bout de l'An's wife is not back home tonight, retaliation will take place tomorrow, first thing in the morning" (Delalande, 221). At 1:30 P.M. the two profoundly discouraged messengers once again take to the road into the Creuse. But they have decided that this will be the last trip. If their mission fails again, they will throw in the towel and remain with the maquis themselves. They return to see "Roger" with their new petition. To arouse some compassion they emphasize the illness of Bout de l'An's little boy, separated from his mother. "Roger" does not offer them a spark of hope but nonetheless goes with them to inform "François." Then he leaves them to wait in Pontarion.

26. The term *Gauleiter* originally designated the Nazi administrative authority responsible for a particular region, or *Gau*, of the Third Reich. Later, *Gauleiters* were designated for the newly created *Gaue* in occupied countries as well.

Meeting with the Surcouf

On June 20 Daniel Blanchard, who is in charge of guarding the hostages, notes that time is passing and that he still has no news concerning them (neither "François" nor "Roger" has kept him informed of the talks in progress). He tells himself that something should be done about these prisoners, who are starting to get used to their routine, and likewise for the hostages taken in Saint-Amand by the militia. And to begin with, perhaps an exact list of this second group should be drawn up. That way, the maquisards will be able to ask for their release in exchange for that of their own prisoners. A visit to Saint-Amand would also give them the chance to deliver a little material help to the families of the maquisards. With this double goal, Blanchard sends his orderly to Saint-Amand. This emissary leaves that very day. For added safety he stops along the way at his in-laws' farm in a neighboring town and has another messenger leave from there. This one goes immediately to Saint-Amand and gets in contact with some resisters who have remained there. Among them is Jarrige. On June 21 they come and find the emissary in his hiding place. They bring him the list of Vichy's hostages, and he in turn presents the aid to go to the families. Then, on the morning of June 22, he heads back to the Creuse.

Provided with this new information, Blanchard calls a staff meeting. Now is the time to establish contact with the militia in Vichy. But Van Gaver wants to submit the matter to the superior leader, "François." On his way to his command post, he runs into "Roger," who informs him, first of all, that a transaction concerning the hostages is already under way and, in addition, that the two emissaries, Delalande and Villatte, are in Pontarion as they speak. Van Gaver immediately turns around and goes back, stops to pick up Blanchard and Le Quellec, and, driven by a chauffeur, the three men hurry off to Pontarion.

Delalande and Villatte have been pacing back and forth for

more than two hours, waiting for "Roger's" return. Suddenly, they notice a black car; four men get out of it. What a surprise it is to recognize the very men that they have been chasing tirelessly since June 10, the leaders of the Resistance fighters of Saint-Amand—and only a few hours before the last ultimatum expires. Van Gaver too is totally surprised to learn that they were sought after by the negotiators. "François" had spoken to him just once, and then only vaguely, of the existence of emissaries from Saint-Amand. By choosing to address himself to "François" rather than the leaders of the Surcouf, "Roger" had caused negotiations (and along with them, the hostages' anguish) to be prolonged by a whole week.

The five men have much to tell each other. For more than an hour the leaders of the Surcouf listen to the story of Delalande and Villatte and come to realize fully the necessity of proceeding to the exchange of hostages. They were already convinced of this anyway; otherwise, their families would be the ones to pay. They then hear a detailed report about family members and mutual friends left behind in Saint-Amand.

"Roger" comes back at this time. While getting out of the car, he shakes his head "no." He approaches them and explains that "François" is thinking in just the way he had supposed he would: the exchange is impossible under the proposed conditions.

Van Gaver and Blanchard do not hesitate for an instant. It is their turn to jump into the car and go off to see "François." The negotiators wait, in anguish. An hour later the leaders of the Sur-couf are back. Van Gaver gets out of the car and nods his head "yes." He was able to plead the case for his town. "Do what you want" is what the Resistance official in the Creuse finally deigned to reply to him (Delalande, 230).

The methods of the exchange are finalized. It is too late to make the exchange that night, so the prisoners will be let go the next morning. A rendezvous is set for 10:00. Van Gaver is a little disap-pointed to discover that the negotiators have room in their car only for the women; he would like also to release a few men who, he realized, did not deserve to be punished. He mentions three of them in particular: Barathon, the mayor of Culan; Bellot, a soldier; and Carion. The latter had left the militia as of December 1943. The others only stayed in a little while and have no crimes on their conscience. It is true that Bout de l'An did not ask that the men be set free, but maybe it is not too late to propose it to him? Of course, an appropriate recompense, a comparable freeing of prisoners, would be demanded. Van Gaver hopes nonetheless that this new exchange will also come to pass.

The negotiators return and go to sleep at the Rateau farm. They are exhausted but, for the first time, relieved.

The Exchange

Lécussan is not one to make jokes, and that is precisely why Bout de l'An chose him to handle the hostage affair. He appeals to the German army, which took position on the outskirts of Saint-Amand in the evening of June 22, ready to begin its reprisal actions. Lécussan's ultimatum expires at 8:00 in the morning, June 23.

At 5:30 A.M., Delalande and Villatte are up. As soon as they are ready, they set out in search of a telephone. At 7:30, Delalande succeeds in waking up a bearded postman in Aigurande and in reaching Lécussan on the line. He announces that the women are in their hands and will arrive in Saint-Amand early in the afternoon; Vichy's hostages must also be brought back. Lécussan agrees to do what is necessary, and the German troops return to their positions.

At 10:00 A.M., Delalande and Villatte are waiting at the intersection of two roads. A black car arrives, and Le Quellec gets out. Then five women, Simone and the four "militiawomen," spring forth from the back seat. They have "over their eyes black blindfolds with purple designs" (Delalande, 235). The blindfolds are removed. There should have been six women. At the last minute one of them, the daughter of a baker, preferred to stay with the maquis rather than have to face the paternal anger resulting from her illicit association with militiamen; after all, life in the maquis is not so bad. Simone takes it upon herself to confirm that the girl failed to come with the others of her own free will. Next, Delalande asks all the women not to reveal anything they have seen. Simone gets in the front seat between him and Villatte, the four others cram themselves into the back, and the car takes off.

On the way, Simone tells the negotiators that she has no complaints about her jailors. She inquires about her children. One of the other passengers is sick, so they stop. Another passenger would like to get out at Châteaumeillant, where her family lives. She is not allowed to do so, but they do make a brief stop in front of her house. Finally, at 1:45 P.M., the car comes to a standstill in front of the subprefecture. Sadrin, Lécussan, and Vigier are waiting for them. They congratulate each other, and Lécussan, probably already drunk, cries tears of joy. Simone is asked what she thinks of her captivity. "I fell into the hands of some people who are nationalists just as much as we are," she answers. "They do not have the same means to the same end, but we should be able to get along with them" (Delalande, 237–38). These words leave Lécussan flabbergasted. Sadrin replies, somewhat ironically: "Well then, Madame, there is some ground worth cultivating there. You ought to devote yourself to the task" (Sadrin, 229).

A meal is offered at the subprefecture, but Simone wishes to leave immediately for Vichy. And where are the hostages from Saint-Amand? "They have not yet arrived," answers Lécussan. Delalande and Villatte look at each other and wonder whether they have made a fool's deal. They guaranteed each party that the two groups of hostages would be released simultaneously. They decide to trust Bout de l'An anyway and to let his wife leave. Actually, they really have no choice. They nevertheless obtain freedom for seven persons held at the post office and Vichy's assurance that the other hostages are in the process of being released.

Bout de l'An does, in fact, keep his word. The hostages from

Saint-Amand will be set free, as will the two wives of Resistance leaders, held at the camp of Gurs. But impatience is growing in Saint-Amand, and people fear the worst: on June 24 the hostages still are not back in spite of repeated promises from Vichy. Finally, on June 25, at 1:00 P.M., the convoy of buses, accompanied by cars of the antiriot police, arrive in town. The hostages are there, safe and sound, including Tahar Kador, arrested while in possession of a weapon; the pharmacist, Chavaillon, minus his hunting rifle; and that dangerous Freemason, retired Colonel Larouquette. In the end all the anguish was avoidable, for if the maquis had not taken hostages, the militia would not have done so either. It seems that everything and everyone have come full circle. But this appearance is deceiving; events have left indelible marks on the minds of the protagonists.

There remains the implementation of the proposal Van Gaver made to release a portion of his men prisoners. Delalande returns to Vichy to talk it over with Bout de l'An and asks that some families of Resistance fighters held by the militia be freed in exchange. Bout de l'An is not opposed to the idea but lets things drag on. For his part, Lécussan does everything in his power to bring about the failure of this new negotiation. He remains convinced that the mediators are spies from the maquis (just as "François" took them for spies from the militia).

Suddenly, dealings with the Creuse region are interrupted. It seems that there is bad news: the German army has reportedly set out to liquidate the maquis who are there.

It is now that destiny will strike its three blows.

PUNISHMENT

Departure of the Surcouf

I t is the beginning of July, and the contact Van Gaver and Blanchard were maintaining with Saint-Amand is interrupted. It becomes clear that they themselves must decide what to do with the detained militiamen.

After the five women are set free (which most of the maquisards hardly hear about), the imprisoned militiamen are twenty in number. They make up a rather disparate group. To clarify the situation, the Resistance fighters have written their names on a big blackboard, hung up on the château. There are the eight defenders of the militia mansion in Saint-Amand, among them the *chef de trentaine*, Bastide, and several former soldiers from the First RI. The latter were captured while in possession of weapons, their political involvement is undeniable, and they themselves are responsible for several human lives since they never hesitated to denounce resisters or hidden Jews to the Gestapo.

Then there are ten other men, arrested during the night of June 6–7. Admittedly, they are militiamen, but they cannot always be accused of specific crimes. Some of them find in the militia a kind of life that is adventurous, exalting, or even heroic, which corresponds to their aspirations. "I would rather live only two years for an ideal than eighty sitting in an armchair doing nothing," affirms one militiamen from Saint-Amand (AD, 755 W 25), thus giving a modern version of the ideal of Achilles, the ancient hero. Certain ones are Pétain supporters; others joined the militia out of pure opportunism: to avoid the STO, to get paid a little money, and to gain self-importance. Still others, young boys, were pushed into it by their parents. For all of that, a few of them regretted it and asked to join the maquis; others, like those mentioned by Van Gaver, deserve to go home. Finally, there are two women, whose presence cannot be explained by politics: the baker's daughter who is afraid of her father, and another, known only by her last name, which is rather surprising for a female friend of the militiamen—she is called the Jewess.

A rather unpleasant episode occurs at this time, which the maquisards do not like to call to mind. One of the militiamen attempts to run away; he is pursued, recaptured, and brought back to camp. A court is instituted, upon which sit ten men, the leaders of the Surcouf. The prisoner is interrogated. He is a physically unattractive human being, somewhat infirm (he walks with a crutch), who never washes himself and so smells bad. No one likes him, not even his fellow captives. A shoe repairman by trade, he admits in the course of interrogation to having denounced thirty-three persons who were subsequently deported to Germany. This Judas was supposedly paid five hundred francs per person sold. He is found guilty and shot to death that same evening. There remains nothing of this man, no particular memory, not even his name. After his death, only nineteen militiamen remain.

On Sunday, July 9, the court reconvenes. They decide to summon the Traitor in order to settle things in their own minds. He is brought to the billiard room at the château. They remind him of the comrades betrayed in the past and of the suspicious phone call during the night of June 7–8. The Traitor makes fierce denials, and there is no proof. Blanchard, who is presiding, is not sufficiently convinced of his guilt and decides to free him on the benefit of the doubt but to keep him with them. The Resistance members who testified against the Traitor are disgruntled. Blanchard has a good-heartedness that is not suited to a military official; he is incapable of imagining that others can be any worse than he. If it had been up to a harder man, Lalonnier or even Chaillaud, the outcome would have been the opposite: if in doubt, either would have preferred to kill an innocent man rather than risk the lives of the whole troop.

On July 14 plans have been made to celebrate the national holiday in freedom, for the first time in five years. Festivities are announced in the town of Bourganeuf, whose streets are strung with garlands. The day before, during a ceremony on the grounds where parachute drops were made, "François" promoted Blanchard to captain (Van Gaver, only a lieutenant, is now his subordinate), and other maquisards are decorated. But that evening there is an alert: an ambush must be set up on the road to Tulle because a German convoy is expected. The maquisards place mines on the roadway and hide all around it. The next morning, events occur differently than anticipated. Frightened by British or American planes flying overhead, the German soldiers abandon the main road and find themselves face to face with the maquisards. A fight begins. The Surcouf loses two men, and a third is captured. Chaillaud, who is commanding the ambush, gives the order to withdraw. The proximity of this German convoy is disturbing. In Bourganeuf the garlands are hastily taken down. In Sardent, though, the men of Lalonnier's FTP, now called "first popular regiment of the Berry," are organizing a parade and public dance.

In reality, disturbing news has been coming in to the maquis command for several days. Since July 9 a German column commanded by General Kurt Jesser has been coming back up from the Cantal region toward the north. Its task is to liquidate the maquis of the regions of the Corrèze, the Haute-Vienne, and the Creuse. Thanks to a good intelligence system, the maquis are kept informed of its progress. But not everyone is afraid of it. "François,"

for example, thinks that the "Bourganeuf-Guéret-Aubusson triangle" is impregnable. Precious days go by: July 15, July 16. Long con-
sultations are held, but no decision is made.

During the night of July 16–17, Jesser's units invest the region of
Bourganeuf, then of Pontarion, where "François" is. At the last
minute he manages to escape from his hideout. He immediately
sends messages to all detachments of maquisards stationed in the
region so that they can clear out as quickly as possible. This decision is in line with what the leaders of the Surcouf were hoping
for: they think they will be more at ease if they return to the Cher,
which they know much better and where they can count on the
locals' complicity.

Preparations for departure are made rapidly. First, it is decided
that the company must be split up into three units. One platoon
will leave with a small truck and head for the Cher. Three other
platoons, with Blanchard and Van Gaver, accompanied by the
other truck drivers and the staff—in all, nearly ninety men—will
depart on foot for the Cher. Finally, the fifth platoon, commanded by Chaillaud, will keep the heavy artillery (that is to say, the
two machine guns); this group of about thirty men will return
more slowly, in small stages. Rendezvous is set for the locality of
L'Abbaye des Pierres, about ten kilometers south of Culan.

The prisoners also are divided into three groups. The two
women and a man judged not to be part of the militia are entrusted to a group of maquis from the Creuse that is staying put,
with the recommendation to release them at the first appropriate
moment. Three other men say they want to fight along with the
Surcouf, and Blanchard takes them with him. So that leaves thirteen, to be guarded by Chaillaud, who, at any rate, is advancing
less quickly.

Late in the afternoon of July 17 the Surcouf leaves Mérignat,
which had given it shelter for more than a month. But a few kilometers away, just past the bridge of Murat, the trucks stop. Here
they will be camouflaged and temporarily abandoned. Though

disappointed, the maquisards understand that it is only prudent to do so. The Blanchard group immediately leaves, going north. They are all loaded down with munitions, provisions, and other items, and do not advance quickly. They stop soon afterward to spend the night.

The next morning they leave again. One detachment goes to the village of Bétête. German soldiers are there, shots ring out, and two Resistance fighters are killed. Blanchard and Van Gaver march at the head of the company. After a few hours Van Gaver starts to limp. He is from the city and is not used to forced marches. In the afternoon Blanchard stops to spend the night in a little wooded area delimited by two lanes. It is the locality of La Croix de la Mine, in the woods of Chauverne, two kilometers from the village of Saint-Dizier-Leyrenne. A few men are sent to get two sheep and some vegetables from the neighboring farms. The others collapse on the spot, exhausted from the march. It is their second night in the woods.

Death and Deportation

In the aftermath of a catastrophe, hindsight always provides a host of signs that foreshadowed it. After the disastrous day of July 19, the resisters will recall that someone had spoken of a suspicious flare during the night, of a young boy who had visited them in the evening before disappearing mysteriously, that it had been recommended to them that they not go in the direction they took. But these insignificant incidents turn into eloquent omens only after misfortune has occurred.

At 6:00 in the morning, the maquisards begin to wake up. But they do not leave right away, for Van Gaver and another resister have gone to get some bread and milk. Suddenly, at 6:45, they hear shots. A few seconds later, they see that other maquisards who had spent the night not far from there are running: they are apprentices from the école de la Garde. They yell, "Run for it! The Germans are on our ass!" The gunfire gets closer, and a first man, who is hit in the head, rolls on the ground.

The leaders of the Surcouf try to organize a defense; enemy fire is answered with the machine guns, and a few grenades are thrown. The attackers fire explosive bullets, hardly appropriate to the circumstances; they strike tree branches, pulverize in the air, and a snowy powder spreads over the maquisards lying on the ground. However, there are also some mortar shells that cause terrible damage. The woods where the maquisards slept form a triangle. The attackers have set up their machine guns on one of the sides and are advancing from the opposite side, driving the maquisards toward the firing line. Blanchard observes that the forces are far too unequal, so the only solution is to "run for your life." The order is passed on to the troops, and a retreat begins. Suddenly, the enemy fire breaks off. A few minutes tick by in agonizing silence, and then the soldiers rush forth only ten meters ahead of the maquisards. Their faces blackened and their helmets camouflaged, they are carrying hand-held machine guns and shouting incomprehensibly (they are Ukranians from the "Vlassov Army," a name that now covers ex-Soviets who are simple mercenaries in the service of the Germany). Blanchard and a few others have distanced themselves a bit but are without cover. Blanchard is wounded; he knows he is doomed. He cries out, "I'll get my Kraut before I die!" The sacrifice that he had accepted on May 31 is in the process of being carried out. He puts one knee to the ground and begins firing his Thompson; he is killed immediately thereafter.

Other men throw their guns to one side, their firing pins to the other. Grenades still hang from their belts, cartridges still cover their stomachs, but all resistance has become useless. They put their hands up. Amid the shouts of the German officers and with their hands now crossed on their heads, they are pushed toward a clearing and stripped of their jackets. The enemy soldiers finish off those who are on the ground wounded. Among the resisters are two Jewish brothers from Alsace, the Mays. Gilbert is wounded; his brother has time to bandage him and put him back on his feet before the soldiers approach them. They remain that way for hours in the dreadful heat, expecting to be executed from one moment to the next. A thought crosses their mind, perhaps: they are paying for what they did six weeks earlier; this is "the dead end to which the liberation of Saint-Amand has led" (Perrot, 48).

The soldiers now comb the nearby woods in search of fugitives. Van Gaver and his companion are killed by a mortar blast near the Villatte farm. A few maquisards manage to hide in a field of rye; another conceals himself at the bottom of a ditch. Three persons have buried themselves under some thick brambles and are keeping still a few meters away from their pursuers. The hours pass; they hold their breath. Toward 11:00 chance betrays them: a soldier steps on the calf of one of them; he pulls him from his hiding place and discovers the two others next to him.

At noon those being held are lined up single file, and the soldiers decide to leave. What is left of the Surcouf? Nine persons are dead and sixty-two under arrest, to which three militiamen who had chosen to go with the Resistance fighters are added; about fifteen maquisards have succeeded in running away. The prisoners are led toward some trucks and cars parked on a small road not far away. They are taken to Bourganeuf and locked up in the town hall. The soldiers step aside now and put them in the hands of the SS. They are subjected to a summary interrogation: identity, locations of weapons stashes, names of leaders. The maquisards have been told that, rather than saying they are in the Resistance, they should answer, "Churchill Mobilization." In passing, they are hit a few times with the butt of a rifle. It is at this time that Le Quellec, the only FFI officer among the survivors, takes it upon himself to reveal to the police the identity of the three militiamen accompanying them so that they might be let go. The militiamen have not asked for this on their own initiative, but Le Quellec

thinks that even if this declaration has the disadvantage of desig-
nating himself as the leader, they must not be made to endure the
fate of all the others. The militiamen are released; the others are
lined up in the courtyard. The neighboring houses are made to
close their shutters. Are they going to be executed at this time? An
officer arrives and announces that the execution is postponed until the next morning at 5:00. They are then directed to a medieval
tower right next door, formerly a prison: the Zizime Tower, thus
named because of its first official occupant, an Ottoman prince
that the Christians call Zizime, a fifteenth-century hostage. It has
lost all of its medieval splendor, and its little rooms smell musty.

The imprisoned Resistance fighters are tormented by the announcement of the impending execution, by hunger—they have
not eaten anything since morning—and especially by thirst. The
night brings no relief. A few of them, having found a piece of a
broken bottle, urinate in it and moisten their lips with their urine.
Others write their names and the date on the wall to leave behind
some trace of themselves. They wonder why the German soldiers
were able to find them; could it be that they had informers? Betrayal is a constant obsession with the resisters; it allows them to
resolve many problems.

On July 20, at 5:00 in the morning, they are checked on but left
in their cells. Not until 9:00 are they made to go down into the
courtyard. A few of them throw themselves against the mossy
green wall of the urinals in order to lick them. Moved by this, the
SS then bring them a cup of water per person. Then they go back
up into the tower. More waiting. Several hours go by. In the early
afternoon some trucks wrapped in barbed wire arrive. The prisoners are crowded inside and leave for an unknown destination.
In certain trucks the German soldiers give them a bit of bread.

That evening they arrive in Aubusson, where they are locked
up on the premises of the trade school. That is where the soldiers
take everyone they arrest in the course of this vast combing operation. The maquisards stay there for three days; their treatment

eases up a bit, and representatives of the Red Cross visit them. They are guarded by some Czechoslovakians who, like them, are hoping for the imminent collapse of the Reich. Their guards reassure them: they will not be shot to death; agreements have been reached between the Allies and the Wehrmacht so that the resisters will be treated as prisoners of war. And they will not be deported: the resisters are blowing up trains; nothing is running anymore. Besides, there is talk of an attempted assassination against Hitler; he may already be dead. The resisters regain hope. One of them, whose arm was mutilated at La Croix de la Mine, is taken to the hospital for an amputation. Although two soldiers guard the door of the operating room, he manages, with the help of some doctors and nurses, to get away by jumping out the window. Two others find an opportunity to run away when they are alone with an unarmed German sergeant, to whom they are explaining how the gasogenes work. But the sergeant makes sure they understand that if they run off, he himself will be executed, as will twenty of their comrades. The spirit of solidarity prevails over self-interest: André Bodain and François Briandet decide to stay.

On July 23 they get back into the trucks. The roads of the Massif central are winding, and they hope that this is the moment that their comrades who were not taken have chosen to liberate them. Yet nothing happens. The batallions led by "François" seem to have vanished into the wild. A few days later his staff will issue a rather fanciful communiqué: "Much fighting has occurred in a great many places. More than 400 Germans have been killed; a great number are wounded; five are now prisoners. FFI losses are climbing to about fifty killed and 178 prisoners. All FFI units are ordered to camouflage themselves and wait" (Parrotin, 458).

They arrive in a big town that some of the prisoners recognize as Clermont-Ferrand. They are led to the Gestapo offices where they undergo another interrogation. One of the resisters named Champion, a former medical student at the University of Strasbourg, recognizes the interpreter as his old professor, a bilingual

Alsatian. The medical school has been evacuated to Clermont. Indignant, Champion directs remarks to him in German so that the Gestapo officers can understand him. "I prefer being in my place to being in yours," he declares, for like Socrates, he would rather suffer injustice than inflict it.

Although they are harassed by the militiamen, the prisoners have better accommodations than in the Zizime Tower. They are still hoping for the announcement of the final collapse of the Reich, which is decidedly long in coming. On July 25 they board a train. The trip is interrupted many times. Nevertheless, by evening they have arrived at their destination, Dijon. The militiamen hand them over to German soldiers. "We bring you crime's army!" they declare, beaming. The German commandant, a bald officer, does not appear to share their enthusiasm and does not even respond to the Nazi salute. "Criminals, criminals everywhere," he answers, "even among those bringing in the others." It was just a little remark, one of the prisoners remembers, but it meant a lot.

They remain locked in these barracks until July 29 and begin to be hopeful once again. On that particular day, however, they are made to board cattle cars that leave for the east. During the night of August 2–3, the sixty-one surviving members of the Surcouf step off of the train. They are in Germany. There is no longer any hope of a speedy release. They will be separated shortly afterward and will soon join the masses of deportees at Buchenwald, Dora, Neuengamme, and Mauthausen.

Execution of the Militiamen

The other maquisards from Saint-Amand meet a different fate. Lalonnier's FTP also discovers that Colonel Jesser's detachment has arrived. They leave their encampments on July 20 and head north. The German and Ukranian soldiers are close by, but the maquisards avoid skirmishes with them. They benefit from the assistance of two young women who have joined with them: Alix, a tall blonde, and Jeannine. The two women circulate freely and guide the men with precision. Following some smaller departmental roads, they manage to make their way out of this region, which has turned into a trap, and on July 26 they settle on the outskirts of Urciers, in the Indre region, where they pursue their resistance activities.

The third group, Chaillaud's, is about thirty-five men strong. In addition there are the thirteen captive militiamen. After separating from Blanchard on the morning of July 18, they temporarily stay where they are, right in the forest of Mérignat. Yet an identical chain of events seems to be set in motion shortly afterward: during the night of July 18–19 the enemy soldiers advance, and the maquisard sentries put out an alert. Awakened, Chaillaud gives the order to "run for your life." The woods are thicker in this area, however, and his men are more spread out. Still, they somehow avoid being surrounded, taking with them, as always, their machine guns and their prisoners. They meet at the Quoirs farm, a few kilometers southwest of their initial location. There they hear the news that the Surcouf has been surrounded and wiped out. They are not happy. Their movement is slow; this large group of people has to be fed, and the enemy soldiers are everywhere.

The next morning, July 20, some maquisards are busy cooking a pot of beans when they see several soldiers stop in front of the farm. The order is given to leave immediately and silently. They manage to get away without being seen. The German detachment is coming from the southwest; the maquisards figure that the best way to hide would be to go precisely in that direction and end up in the spot that the others have already left. They therefore head for Saint-Léonard-de-Noblat in the Haute-Vienne region. They do not know exactly where they are because all they have for a compass and a map is a post office calendar.

After marching for several hours they make a stop in the woods.

Chaillaud then calls his comrades together and tells them the conclusion he has reached: the militiamen must be executed. By some miracle the resisters have just escaped two encirclements, but luck will perhaps fail to smile upon them a third time. The German soldiers are very close by; a shout from one of the militiamen is all it would take for all of them to be discovered, and for the Resistance fighters to be wiped out. Transporting the prisoners and taking care of them is a task beyond their means. The prisoners cannot be released, either, first, because they are considered guilty, and second, because they know only too well the identity and the hiding places of the maquisards. Chaillaud was not happy to make this decision, but it is a vital one—it is necessary to their survival.

What makes the decision dramatic is that the militiamen and maquisards now know each other. A month and a half of life together has transformed abstract enemies into rather pitiable individuals. Moreover, in many cases, guards and detainees have had frequent association since childhood, attended school together, and dated the same girls. Often it was pure chance that oriented some toward the militia and others toward the maquis. Chaillaud is well acquainted with the leader of the militia, Louis Bastide. Both are from Saint-Amand. It is even said that Bastide did Chaillaud a favor one day: Chaillaud was under arrest and about to be interrogated when Bastide walked by him and said, "The interrogation could go on a long time, so go to the bathroom beforehand." Chaillaud caught the meaning of the suggestion and, in the bathroom, emptied his pockets. When nothing was found on his person, he was released. Now it is his turn to decide the destiny of Bastide.

Some maquisards approve of Chaillaud's reasoning; others express their disagreement. But the decision has been made, and it must be implemented right away. Here is Chaillaud's account, given in 1967, concerning the death of the prisoners:

We couldn't shoot the militiamen; the Germans would have heard the detonations. We hanged them. We made slipknots with parachute cords which we tied to big branches. We had neither a stool nor a chair. We placed the slipknots around their necks, we lifted them up as high as possible, and we let them fall. The militiamen died courageously. When I told their leader that they were going to be executed, he simply said to me, "You relied on England and we relied on Germany; you won and we lost." (Delperrié, 2:108)

The argument that consists of systematically opposing the British and the Germans was common among the militiamen, so it is plausible in this context. On the other hand, it seems that Chaillaud may have wished to embellish the death of the militiamen's leader, perhaps out of unconscious gratitude for the good deed that had been done for him. According to other accounts, Bastide actually got down and begged that his life be spared.

Thus "relieved" of their burden, the maquisards follow Chaillaud and go off again in the direction of the Cher. It takes them eight days to reach the rallying point, the Abbaye des Pierres, on the outskirts of Culan. Some of them, disgusted or traumatized by what just happened, abandon the maquis and go back home.

Roundup of the Jews

Rural Berry has no notable Jewish minority. Aside from Deputy Mayor Lazurick (himself "parachuted in" from Paris), there were only two well-known Jewish families in Saint-Amand before the war, those of two manufacturers; within the region as a whole there were a few merchants and hotel keepers. But in 1939–1940, Saint-Amand attracted refugees: it was a medium-size town, more or less centrally located in the heart of an agricultural region in the Free Zone, and most important, we should remember that it was a quiet spot where nothing ever happened. These refugees basically came from two parts of France, Alsace-Lorraine, which was now German, and the Paris region. For a certain number of them this was not the first time they had fled. They had been born in Poland, Russia, or Rumania, and it was during the 1920s or 1930s that they made their way to the land of the rights of man. In all, about fifty Jewish families settled in Saint-Amand.

These people, most of whom were of modest means, worked and tried to create a favorable image of themselves. A report by Subprefect Dutilleul-Francoeur addressed to René Bousquet in July 1942 described them this way: "Disciplined as a whole, their main preoccupation seems to be to go unnoticed by the civil authorities" (AD, M. 7298). They nonetheless became victims of two big roundups, that of August 26, 1942, carried out in the wake of the roundup at the Vél' d'Hiv in Paris, and that of February 23–24, 1943. The first one entailed the deportation of thirty-seven people; the second, thirty-five (although Vichy had called for only twenty-five). The Jews rounded up were selected on the basis of very precise criteria; indeed, there were painstakingly detailed regulations that established what might be called the degree of deportability. In the Free Zone, Jews who were French citizens were theoretically not deportable. In the case of foreigners, deportation could be deferred if the person in question had a French spouse or French children, had served in the French army, was more than sixty years old, or was seriously ill (the pretense of work camps was maintained).[27] Pregnant women were exempted. Men between the ages of eighteen and forty were the first to be deported, starting with single men, then those who were married but without children, and finally, those with families. Converts to Catholicism had a better chance of staying than those who practiced their own religion. Although these deportations did take place, approximately two hundred Jews still lived in Saint-Amand after the second roundup.

27. To hide from the French public the real fate of those being deported, government authorities informed the populace that the deportees were heading for work camps in the east.

During the summer of 1943 the subprefecture tried to force the Jews to leave town—first those who did not have a job in Saint-Amand, then those who had family in another town within the department, and finally the others—on the pretext that the town needed their housing as officers' quarters for the newly created First RF. Those who could move to the country did so willingly. However, a good number did not leave. The police were not very strict, and in addition, the employee in charge of Jewish affairs at the subprefecture was a resister who tried to warn the threatened families.

When the town was taken over on June 6, some young men of Jewish origin joined with the insurgents; the rest made themselves scarcer than ever. The mother of Georges Kiejman[28] (who at the time was a student at the Saint-Amand high school) immediately withdrew her son from school and kept him under wraps at home, in the country. In troubled times it was not wise for Jews to be seen very much. But at this early stage there was no new persecution.

Things began to change for the worse when Lécussan moved into the subprefect's office. With him, anti-Semitism is an obsession. He brought along with him his lieutenant, André Rochelet, with whom he had attended the anti-Semitic conference of Berlin and assigned him the responsibility of handling Jewish questions in Saint-Amand. Rochelet and Marchand updated the lists of names of all Jews living in the town. On June 29, Rochelet arrested the Juda family, longtime residents of the region: two brothers, the wife of one of them, and the daughter of the other. This arrest was part of a roundup planned by Lécussan in retaliation for the murder of Philippe Henriot, state secretary for information and propaganda and militiaman. He was convinced that the Jews paid to have Henriot killed and thought that at least one thousand of them should be executed. In the meantime he has designated the Judas as hostages (and at the same time helped himself to their

28. The lawyer and politician Georges Kiejman was a minister in the government of President François Mitterrand.

wine cellar: about fifty bottles of good vintage wine). On July 17, at Lécussan's request, the family will be transferred to the Bordiot prison in Bourges. This is a dangerous location because this prison is under the direct control of the Gestapo. There they will join another Jew, Dr. Mojzesz Seiden, under arrest since May 24 (he is an FTP official from Blancafort).

Back in Saint-Amand, on July 12, the body of Félix May is fished out of the Berry canal. May was president of the local chapter of the UGIF, the Vichy organization that grouped Jews together, and father of the two May brothers who went off with the Resistance. His sons are held responsible for the death of two militiamen, Patin and Parmène, on June 6, living proof of the collusion between Jewry and communism. In compliance with another order from Lécussan, the father was tortured in the offices of the militia before being shot in the head several times and thrown into the canal.

In the afternoon of July 20, Lécussan receives a telephone call informing him of the execution of the militiamen in the Creuse region. This call comes just a few hours after their death; who could have placed it? A curious coincidence would seem to point the finger at the person I have designated as the Traitor. Indeed, he was with Chaillaud until that day; he has not been seen since July 20, and he never again returns to Saint-Amand, not even after the war. One detail: the message announces the death of eight militiamen, not thirteen, as if the person sending it had attended only part of the execution (or as if Lécussan were thinking of the eight *franc-gardes* arrested at the mansion where the militia were staying). This figure of eight will also appear in the first account of the execution, recorded after the Liberation.

Upon hearing this news, Lécussan flies into a blind rage. He had never looked favorably on the talks Bout de l'An engaged in with the maquisards, which certainly allowed the leader to recover his wife but which at the same time lent a semblance of respectability to the loathsome terrorists. Lécussan never refrained from exhibiting his hostility toward the negotiators and from throwing a wrench into the works. He was not really satisfied when the exchange was carried out, even though he was moved by Simone's return. The affront suffered by the militia—the takeover of the town and the arrest of some of his men—has never been avenged. Adding insult to injury, the maquisards now commit yet another crime: they take the liberty of killing eight militiamen, taking advantage of the impunity that distance affords them. Lécussan has always believed that every blow must be answered, with added force if possible. That is his conception of honor and dignity. The maquisards are inaccessible—for the moment—but that does not make them invulnerable. As is always the case with reprisals, he will strike those who are handy and for some reason considered to be accomplices of the truly guilty. In Lécussan's mind there is a group within the population that is, so to speak, intrinsically guilty: the Jews. Even if they did not personally participate in the events of June 6 and 7, the now remote cause of the execution of the militiamen, these events are the outgrowth of the Jewish, cosmopolitan, and Communist mind. Besides, the whole Resistance movement is paid for with Jewish money. And to make them expiate the insult sustained by the militia, the usual reprisal is called for, taking ten of them for one, or eighty in all.

The militiamen of Saint-Amand risk not being up to the task, and in any case, during the times when he emerges from his drunken state, Lécussan thinks of being "covered" by those above him. But rather than ask Bout de l'An, his superior in the militia, whom he suspects is lacking in backbone, he decides to call on those whose answer he can already predict. He thus telephones Paoli at the Gestapo in Bourges (more precisely, at the SD, or Sicherheitsdienst).

Pierre-Marie Paoli is a young man who was born in the Cher; his father, a man of humble social standing, had been brought up by Child Welfare. Under the influence of some friends professing collaborationist ideas, he got himself hired by the Gestapo at Bourges in March 1943, where he worked as an interpreter (he could speak some German). He then discovered that the shame and humiliation he had experienced as an adolescent were soothed by the power he enjoyed in his position with the Gestapo. In fact, his enterprising spirit quickly transformed him into someone much more important than a simple interpreter: instead of attending interrogation and torture sessions and merely translating the painfully elicited confessions, he took charge of the prisoners personally. His knowledge of the countryside and his powers of seduction with women (he has the good looks of a Latin lover) added to his effectiveness. The Resistance began to suffer the effects of his actions. For this reason, the FTP of the Cher decided to do away with him. They attempted an assassination on August 15, 1943, but Paoli escaped with a wound to the stomach. He spent three months recuperating before returning to the Gestapo at Bourges. At that point he unleashed his fury: the number of arrests multiplied, always followed by torture sessions of the worst sort and thus, by confessions, then by new arrests, and finally by deportations or executions. The list of Paoli's victims is long and impressive; single-handedly (with the help of the Gestapo machine, of course) he managed to seriously hinder Resistance activities throughout the province.

Lécussan explains his plan to Paoli: to use the Jewish population of Saint-Amand to avenge the events of June 6 and 7 and their consequences. Paoli (who came to Saint-Amand on June 8, on the heels of the German Army) refers the matter to his superior, the Gestapo chief of Bourges, Erich Hasse. In turn, Hasse consults his regional superior in Orléans, Fritz Merdsche. The latter approves the operation. In the evening, Paoli calls Lécussan back and settles the details of the roundup with him. It is to take place the next night, and eighty people will be arrested. In an unusual move the curfew is moved up to 10:00 P.M.. Lists are established by Lécussan with the help of his lieutenants, Rochelet and Marchand. But it seems that someone has leaked information (several Resistance sympathizers work at the subprefecture); certain Jewish families were warned and have had time to go and hide.

Early in the afternoon of July 21, a convoy leaves Bourges for Saint-Amand. Forty German soldiers board a bus. They are accompanied by some private cars whose passengers are Gestapo employees, among whom are Hasse and Paoli. Following them are about fifteen militiamen from Bourges, led by their chief, Roger Thévenot.

The convoy arrives in Saint-Amand around 4:00 P.M. and is met by Lécussan. For his part, Lécussan has called together all available militiamen. This group, about one hundred in all, gathers at the Rex movie theater, which never resumed showing films after June 4 but has withstood attempts to blow it up with dynamite. Now, a month and a half after the Allied landing, it can once again serve as headquarters. Lécussan holds forth to his troops, announcing the vengeance that is now possible for the affront of June 6 (he avoids talking about the militiamen who were hanged) and the arrest planned for eighty Jews. He has also ordered that three trucks be requisitioned, anticipating the spoils they will accrue that night. The leaders—Hasse and the other Gestapo officials, Paoli, Thévenot, Lécussan, Marchand, Rochelet—then retire to the best hotel and restaurant in town. Lécussan distributes the list of Jews to arrest with their addresses, neighborhood by neighborhood. Groups of about ten people are formed, each composed of French militiamen and German soldiers. Also summoned are four police agents from Saint-Amand, to ensure that the addresses are located without delay. Then a huge meal is ordered, with a copious amount of wine. At 10:00 P.M. the leaders leave to meet their troops at the Rex. The special intervention squads are instructed about their duties, and the roundup begins. At 11:00 P.M. they are knocking on the first doors.

When the sound of voices awakens Mr. and Mrs. Brunschwig around midnight, there are already twenty militiamen and German soldiers inside their home. "You are under arrest. You are being taken to a camp." This is an unlikely fabrication, for the husband, age seventy-three, is not allowed to take either his dentures or his glasses, nor is he allowed even to get dressed; he leaves wearing his pajamas. He is tripped and falls flat on the ground in front of the truck. His wife is authorized to get dressed, in front of the militiamen, who take this time to help themselves to the things inside the drawers. She sees the house next door, where they arrest Mr. Jeankelowitsch, the owner of a store, and his wife. The half-paralyzed man is pulled by his feet and dragged on his back, to be thrown like a piece of freight onto the waiting truck.

At about 1:00 in the morning, an insistent ringing of their doorbell wakes up the Salomon family. The door is broken down at the same moment, and thirteen men come bursting into the room. They arrest the father, the mother, and their ten-year-old daughter, and they confiscate all their goods, including the child's piggy bank.

Shortly before 4:00 A.M. the doorbell wakes up another family: Lucien Kahn; his wife; their two daughters; their nephew, Marcel Walewyk, who is visiting them on vacation; and their grandson Patrick, three and a half years old. There is no listening to their explanations and their protests; everyone must leave. Patrick's mother would like to take with her a few sewing supplies, but she is told: "That won't be necessary, we're taking you to Paradise" (*La Tragédie de Guerry*, 42).

At about 11:30 P.M. the door of Charles and Marthe Krameisen is broken down by blows from rifle butts. Born in Poland, the Krameisens have lived since the 1920s in the area around Metz, where they met, got married, and now run a small business. They arrived in Saint-Amand in 1939. Although they are foreigners, they were not taken in the previous roundups since their two children are French. They nevertheless sent their children to the country, for added security. The Krameisens sleep on the second floor, above their clothing shop. Charles tries to get away; he runs to the attic and hides behind some old furniture. The soldiers and militiamen who have already seized his wife discover him soon afterward. They strike him violently; his face is bloodied, and he cannot see a thing. One of the soldiers aims his gun at him, but his wife steps in between them: "Why do you want to kill him? He only hid because he was afraid." The soldier lowers his gun, but the militiaman next to him says, "We need to tie this dog up because he will run away." He pulls the man's hands behind his back and handcuffs them, then pushes him into the truck.

Colonel Fernand Bernheim, a veteran of World War I, age seventy-six, is completely dressed, as if he were waiting for this visit (he used to live in the same hotel in which the militia had dinner a few hours earlier). To the militiamen who arrest him he says, "You have sunk to a new low in coming to arrest me" (*La Tragédie de Guerry*, 14).

Léon Weil, a veteran, a released prisoner of war and Alsatian, took refuge in Saint-Amand in the care of his brother-in-law, Lucien Kahn. In August 1943, at the time when housing was being requisitioned, he had to move to a nearby village. On July 6, 1944, he was arrested by Marchand and locked up in the Saint-Amand post office. During the night of July 21–22 they think of him and at about midnight he is led to the Rex, as is another Jewish prisoner.

It is there, indeed, that the trucks unload their cargo. At about 4:00 A.M. the roundup is over. Little by little, all the people arrested in the course of the night file into the damaged movie theater. A count is taken: seventy-six in all, twenty-eight men, thirty-eight women, and ten children, including an eleven-month-old baby; one of the men had already been a hostage in Vichy. The total is not far off the figure of eighty that was set in advance by Lécussan, although a few individuals still succeeded in hiding themselves. For several more hours militiamen and German policemen continue to pillage homes now vacated by their occupants. Among those who have stayed to guard the Jews, the militiamen are markedly more brutal than the Gestapo agents. To try to re-cover his papers, which were confiscated, Léon Weil goes to see Rochelet, who answers him derisively: "You won't be needing them now" (*La Tragédie de Guerry*, 38). Weil understands what it is that awaits him and decides to try his luck. Being well ac-quainted with the Rex, he remembers the existence of a hidden door that leads to the café next door. He takes advantage of a mo-ment of inattention by the guards and slips outside. He then finds himself in a courtyard, scales a wall, inadvertently breaks a win-dow, jumps down into another courtyard, and presents himself to the people living there, asking them to hide him. He will stay with them throughout the whole next day. The day after that, at 5:00 in the morning, he will be led to a maquis hideout outside town. He is not the only one to think of fleeing, but he is one of the few who are alone. The others were taken by whole families, and the pres-ence of young children or elderly parents paralyzes the able-bod-ied men and women. A few people do, however, manage to con-vince the Gestapo officers present that they are pure "Aryans," even though their spouses are Jewish: a man, three women, and a baby are released.

At 7:00 in the morning of July 22, the seventy remaining de-tainees are taken out and loaded again onto the requisitioned trucks. The twenty-six men get on the first one, the women and children on the second one. Since there is a lack of space, Hasse, who is commanding, says, "Pack them in like sardines, and if nec-essary, get rid of the bags" (*La Tragédie de Guerry*, 42). Kahn's daughter, Mrs. Charley, throws her little boy inside and hurries on after him, stepping on other people's bodies. A third truck contains some of the previous night's booty, the rest having gone to the mili-tia of Saint-Amand. The soldiers get back on their bus, the officers get in the cars, and the convoy heads for Bourges. The militiamen of Saint-Amand return to their "little fort," telling those who had remained there, "That's that, all the Jews are under arrest" (Delperrié, 2:111). They open the bottles of wine and spirits that they have just confiscated and amuse themselves by shooting their guns off into the air.

At 9:00 A.M. the convoy stops in the yard of the Bordiot prison. The prisoners are let off the trucks and counted. Only seventy? "Haven't you lost a few on the way?" asks the Gestapo officer. "We will surely lose a few more," laughs Hasse (*La Tragédie de Guerry*, 41). All are meticulously frisked, and their goods are confiscated, after which they are confined without food until 7:00 P.M. in the prison exercise yard, a sort of pen with wire fencing around it. It is very hot; the children cry. Then the prisoners are told that transfer to the camp has been delayed. They will spend the night crowded into cells, the men separated from the women.

The Wells of Guerry

On July 23, Hasse telephones his superior, Merdsche, in Orléans. He reports on the success of the operation of the night before. At the same time, though, he finds the presence of these seventy Jews a bit burdensome. The prison is overcrowded, and he does not want to have responsibility for them. But transferring them to Drancy[29] has become problematic because the railroad lines have been sabotaged, and maquisards are everywhere. What should he do about it? Merdsche answers that transferring them to the camps in the east has indeed become impossible; but as he is well informed of the destiny of those who are sent there, he knows the solution to the problem: the Jews must be eliminated on site by Hasse and his subordinates.

Thus, it is Merdsche who makes the decision to execute the Jews. Is this to say that the other participants of the operation do not bear responsibility for it? When Lécussan decided to arrest

29. During the Occupation, Drancy, a small locality on the outskirts of Paris, was the site of a prison camp in which Jews were held before being sent to other prison camps in France and to the east. Convoys departing from France for Auschwitz originated at Drancy.

eighty Jews, he did so in response to the deaths of eight of his men; so death is what he was thinking of, whether an immediate killing or a deportation with no return. He delivered the Jews to the people he knew he could trust not to let them go. When Hasse and his subordinates, or Paoli and his militiamen, refused to let the Jews take along with them even the articles most necessary for survival, such as dentures or a needle and thread, when they promised them to send them to paradise or to lead them off track on the way, they entertained no illusions as to the fate reserved for their prisoners: it is death, sooner or later, but certain death. Their victims have already crossed the threshold beyond which they can no longer be considered living human beings. The only thing that was not decided was what form their execution will take, and this is precisely the matter that Merdsche has just settled.

Nonetheless, the form of death is no minor detail; and although he has numerous murders on his conscience, Hasse is somewhat troubled by it, if we are to believe Paoli. On his own authority he decides to apply this order only to the men and to spare the women and children. In the afternoon he calls a meeting in his office. In attendance are Emmerich, three other German officers, Paoli, and Thévenot. Hasse explains the situation to them: the order to eliminate the twenty-six Jews, the necessity of doing it with the greatest discretion (the Allied forces are not far off; retreat is now a possibility), and the importance of the action, "a matter of the Reich's safety" (AD, 755, W 1). The execution site is chosen: the military range of Bourges, a vast, uninhabited area used for weapons drills. The date is set: the next day, at 4:00 P.M. Thévenot will furnish transportation, and Paoli will participate in the actual killing.

The prisoners are uncomfortable in the narrow cells in which they have been cooped up since the evening of July 22. Wooden shutters cover the windows, the heat is stifling, and there is only one slop pail per cell for every twenty-four hours (the men are eighteen to a single cell). On July 23 they are fed: dry beans in the morning, another ration in the afternoon. During their walk, their bags are searched, and any precious object they were able to save is taken. Mrs. Charley's ring does not come off her finger quickly enough: "You ate too much in Saint-Amand." She asks what they are planning to do with the children. She is told not to worry, that she will be able to keep her child with her until the end (*La Tragédie de Guerry*, 43). The end?

At 1:00 P.M. on July 24, the small truck procured by Thévenot stops in front of the Bourges prison, and some militiamen get out and rush inside the building. A short time later, Lécussan arrives from Saint-Amand. These are, after all, "his" Jews; he has been kept informed of their fate, and he is coming to demonstrate his consent to the adopted solution: the murder of the Jews. The death of the militiamen will be avenged, and the insult sustained will be avenged with blood. The men detained are called by name, one by one, and the militiamen lead them, along with their meager baggage, to the truck. They are going to be transferred "to the camp," probably at Drancy. The truck can hold a maximum of only about fifteen people, so the twenty-six are literally piled in on top of each other, and they have difficulty breathing. The truck has been covered with a tarpaulin, but the prisoners look through the slits and notice a young man in a German uniform pacing back and forth while nervously smoking a cigarette. It is Paoli.

At 4:30 the Gestapo's black Citroën pulls up. Inside are Emmerich and three subordinates. Paoli gets in next to them, and the two vehicles get going, the truck driven by a militiaman from Orléans. They first take the road to Nevers, the one going east, which somewhat reassures the prisoners; they are surely being taken to a camp. But a short time later they turn right and follow a small road into the military range, amid the brush. A few kilometers farther they stop. Emmerich has caught sight of an excavation, a bomb crater three meters deep, where he thinks it would be possible to throw the Jews' bodies, for it is imperative that the bodies be well camouflaged. There would still be too much work to do to cover the bodies, though. Emmerich and another Gestapo agent then take the car to look for a more appropriate place, leaving their companions behind. Inside the truck the prisoners are beginning to get suspicious about the wait. Are they really being taken to a camp? They do not have time to discuss it for long. Paoli hears their voices, approaches them, and says in his poor German, "No talking here." A half hour later the black car is back, and everyone leaves again.

The execution site chosen is Guerry, an abandoned, isolated farm. Around it are three deep wells that the Gestapo agents have located. The two vehicles come to a stop inside the farmyard, although the truck's engine remains on. The passengers in the car get out and look the place over. The militiaman looks around himself and says happily to Paoli, "It smells bad around here. Great!" The prisoners hear him and are frightened. Still suffering from the rough ride and the lack of space, several of them vomit. The men from the Gestapo choose one of the wells outside the farmyard to be the execution site, 150 meters away from the spot where the prisoners are waiting. With a revolver in hand, Emmerich and Paoli stand on opposite sides of the well. The militiaman is a little off to one side, holding a machine gun just in case anyone tries to get away.

The other Gestapo agents return to the truck. "Six men, with your bags, get off!" one of them orders. The first six get off. They get in line, single file. One Gestapo agent goes in front of them, another one follows behind with his gun in hand, and the third one guards the truck. Outside the farm, on the pathway to the well, lies a pile of rubble, small stones and sacks of hardened cement. Each man is asked to put down his suitcase and carry a stone or a sack on his shoulders. Once at the well, they stop. The first in line must come forward, put down his load and kneel before the low wall of the well, approximately fifty centimeters high. All the Gestapo agents have to do is tip the victim over into the well. Then it is the turn of the second man, who now knows perfectly well what is in store for him but can do nothing about it. Once the six men are at the bottom of the well, the Gestapo agents throw in the stones and sacks of cement. The men die either of asphyxia or from their skulls being crushed.

Barely ten minutes have passed. The escort team is back at the truck. "Six more men, get off!" (Lyonnet, 91). The operation is repeated in identical fashion. Another ten minutes pass; six more men are called. Among these six is Lucien Kahn. His young nephew, Marcel Walewyk, is distraught, does not want to be separated from his uncle, and asks to get off with him. The magnanimous Gestapo agent grants him that favor, so off they go as a group of seven, following the same path.

There now remain only seven men in the truck. One of them is Charles Krameisen. He has heard some suspicious noises — rocks hitting each other — after each group left the truck. He has fewer and fewer doubts concerning the fate awaiting them. He decides to try his luck and attempt an escape. He tried it the first time in his attic; a second time, at the Rex, he did not dare to try it because of the people with him; perhaps the third time will be a charm. He takes off his heavy shoes, which would prevent him from running fast, and just at that moment he hears a faint sort of bang that reminds him of a revolver going off (one of the men in the preceding group tried to run away but too late). One of the prisoners says to him, "You hear? They're shooting," and immediately afterward is overcome by violent trembling. Krameisen then tells his other companions, "I prefer to be killed from behind rather than head on, I will try to get away" (Lyonnet, 91). Another man next to him answers, "Krameisen, it's no use running away, they'll kill you anyway." The others are numb and do not even react.

Heroes prefer to be killed head on rather than from behind. Krameisen is not a hero; he wants to live: for himself, for his wife,

for his children. He is acting in the way Sagnelonge did. Knowing
that he has nothing to lose, he refuses to sit back passively and let
himself be killed.

Ten more minutes go by, and the Gestapo agents are back. "The
rest of you, down here." Krameisen is careful to get off last. He
quickly glances around. The vehicles are standing in the farmyard, which is surrounded by wire fencing. Several buildings are
in a state of ruin, and an old chimney of rusty sheet metal is lying
on the ground. The place is deserted. The grass all around is yellow, scorched from the sun; it has not rained in weeks. The air is
heavy; it is a hot summer afternoon. The Gestapo agents lead the
prisoners out of the farmyard, and one of them says to the other in
German, "Here is where they kill the hares." Krameisen, who understands the language, no longer has the slightest doubt. He tells
himself that this is it and puts his suitcase on the ground. When
the line turns right, in the direction of the well, he begins to run
with all his might ("like a crazy man," he recalls), with bare feet,
to the left. Some thirty meters separate him from the exterior wall
of the farm. His goal is to make it to the wall and go around it.

The Gestapo agents, who are on their fourth round, are caught
off guard by this initiative. The two men at the back of the line
take several seconds to realize what is going on. When they finally shoot, Krameisen has run the distance that separates him from
the corner and has just turned it. The bullets graze the wall. He
throws himself down on his stomach in the bushes that, fortu-
nately, have overrun the grounds, and he hears five or six other
shots. "Tearing my clothes, scraping my skin, gasping, and plagued
by nervous shaking, I slipped like a wild animal from bush to bush,
then copse to copse, until I could consider myself saved" (Lyonnet, 92). One of the Gestapo agents follows him for a minute, fails
to get him, and gives up. The others dare not scatter, for their numbers are not great enough, and other Jews could try to run away.
One of them makes such an attempt and is immediately killed.
Paoli, who has heard the shots, comes back to the truck. The

Gestapo agent who had gone after Krameisen steps forward to meet Paoli and tells him that he succeeded in killing the fugitive and that he threw the body into another well. Was he afraid he would be reprimanded for his negligence, or was he taking advantage of the opportunity to spare the life of this man who had done nothing to him? Paoli comments for his part: "We had no difficulty believing him, or at least we pretended to believe him."

After they have thrown the last bodies and the last bags of cement into the well, the men from the Gestapo return to the farm and hurl the victims' baggage into the well located inside the farmyard. They get in the car once again, and at about 8:00 P.M. they are back home.

Hidden inside a bush, trembling and exhausted, Krameisen tries not to make a sound. It is still daylight at 6:00 P.M. Night falls slowly, and Krameisen notices a searchlight that sweeps through the brush. "For hours at a stretch I remain still, flat on the ground, not daring to cough, with my throat parched." Then he hears a rooster crow and decides to go to the nearest farm. He crawls through the fields, and in the light of the stars he sees some houses. He knocks at the first door. Nobody answers. He then hides in what looks like an abandoned barn. At dawn the owner of the farm comes to get some hay. His name is Camille Guillemin, and he is a poor peasant and father of eight children. He sees before him a bloodied, half-naked little man with a wild look in his eyes, who, in halting French, tells an incomprehensible story. But Guillemin catches the gist of it and drags him inside the house, telling him, "The village is occupied, we both are risking death, you by staying here, me by hiding you. But I will keep you" (*La Tragédie de Guerry*, 18). Krameisen stays on the farm three days, somewhat regains his wits, then goes to hide with some people he knows until the German army pulls out.

In the afternoon of July 24, at the very same time that the small truck is heading for Guerry, the (Catholic) wife of one of the internees and the ("Aryan") fiancée of another appear at the Bordiot prison in Bourges to ask to see their men. "They just left for the camp," they are told.

On July 26, Hasse notices that in his rush he "overlooked" two men in the prison, the Juda brothers. They too fulfill the conditions that were required for the execution of July 24: they are male, from Saint-Amand, and Jewish. Things must be put back into order, and so the men are taken out of prison, led directly to the farm at Guerry and thrown down the third well, also situated outside the estate. No witness has recounted the details of this execution, which is also directed by Emmerich. Paoli denies having had any part in it.

The rescuer of the hostages, Captain Delalande, again tries to obtain freedom for a few of the detainees. Knowing German agencies and their mania for classification, he tries to exploit the law when it is on his side. In late July he thereby manages to bring about the release of two women who are Swiss citizens. He also pleads the case of a French citizen, a veteran, not knowing that the man is already at rest at the bottom of a well at Guerry. He is on his own this time, for none of the other negotiators undertakes any steps to save the lives of the Jews. It is true that they are not really citizens of Saint-Amand, nor are they Catholics.

The advance of the Allies continues, and the active collaborators and the militiamen are becoming more and more disturbed. Paoli leaves Bourges for the east on the night of August 6. Everywhere, people are packing their bags. For its part, the maquis is becoming bolder and bolder. On August 7 at 3:00 P.M., a maquisard kills Roger Thévenot, the chief of Bourges's militia, at point-blank range as he enters the rue Calvin on his way to the headquarters of the militia.

Who decided that Thévenot should be executed? After the war, Lieutenant-Colonel Arnaud de Vogüé, known as "Colomb," head of the FFI of the Cher-Nord region (which oversees Bourges), writes in a document titled "Review of the Armed Resistance in the Cher-Nord": "Around August 10, on orders from me, the head of the militia at Bourges, a man named Thévenot, was shot to death with a revolver at 3:00 in the afternoon, in the center of town. This execution would greatly demoralize the militiamen in his command (approximately two hundred in number) and would apparently contribute to their hasty departure for Germany a week later" (De La Barre de Nanteuil, 47–48).

This brief account, though written shortly after the events, contains numerous inaccuracies. Thévenot was killed on August 7, not August 10. The militiamen from Bourges, as well as those from the rest of France, had by this time reason enough to be demoralized, so the death of their local chief did not add all that much to their discouragement. The order for them to leave is decided elsewhere. Vigier, the regional official, comes to inform them of it the morning of August 8, and by evening of the same day they have left town. The execution of Thévenot has no strategic or military justification; it is a sentence handed down without a trial or deliberation. Finally, it was not de Vogüé who gave the order for the execution.

In his memoirs, a former Resistance fighter, Roger Bardy, known as "Berry," says:

A man posing as a maquisard was arrested on August 8 [a slip of his memory; the date is August 7]. "Alex," "Murat" and "Berry" order him to kill the head of the militia of the Cher (Thévenot) in order to save his own life. The pseudo-maquisard carries out this order and, at 3:00, Thévenot is killed on the rue Calvin in Bourges, thereby depriving the enemy of a valuable auxiliary. The pseudo-maquisard was given amnesty and later became a true resister (Rafesthain, 229–30).

The maquisard chiefs suspect one of their own men, and they give him a brutal choice: perish by their bullets or prove his loyalty by killing Thévenot. He hastens to give the proof demanded of him and transforms himself from a pseudo-maquisard into a real one.

For the "enemy," the militiamen are at this time not so much "valuable auxiliaries" (in view of what operations? — the Germans are already being put to rout) as they are a cumbersome weight.

But the Gestapo cannot simply overlook the affront it suffered in the murder of one of its collaborators. Hasse makes a quick decision: the usual proportion will be applied; they will kill ten for one. It is true that he has no more Jewish men at hand at the prison, but that does not matter. They will draw from the next category, that of women with no children. Hasse no longer even asks for Merdsche's opinion in Orléans since the general directives issued by Merdsche were very clear.

At 7:00 P.M. the German interpreter Müller (Paoli is no longer there) appears at the Bordiot prison, goes into the women's cell, and asks ten of them, women without children, to get ready for the next morning. "You will be going to a camp," he tells them. Of these women, three actually do have children, although they are hidden in the country, but their mothers preferred not to reveal their existence. In particular, this is the case of Marthe Krameisen, who has a boy and a girl.

On August 8 at 8:00 A.M. the ten women find themselves back in the prison yard. Two of them, Mrs. Brunschwig and Mrs. Klein, are Catholics married to Jews. Mrs. Brunschwig has asked since being arrested that they verify her papers attesting that she is an "Aryan" and a Catholic, but no one has listened to her: "We'll see at the camp." As she boards the truck, she is weeping and protesting. A Gestapo officer approaches, and a conversation between him and the soldier guarding the women ensues.

"What's wrong with this woman?"

"She's nuts."

Luckily for her, Mrs. Brunschwig speaks good German and is able to break into the conversation, saying, "I am not nuts, I am not Jewish and I should not be deported" (*La Tragédie de Guerry*, 39–40). The officer makes her get off the truck, and Mrs. Klein as well, and promises to come back the next day to verify their papers. The two women go back to their cell.

The eight others remain in the truck. At this point a man is brought forth. It is Dr. Seiden, who has been languishing in prison for more than two months. He is a Resistance fighter, it is true, and he even participated in the assassination attempt against Paoli, but he is also a Jew, and a clean sweep of the place must be made. The truck takes off in the direction of Guerry. No one has told what torture these nine individuals suffered. Their dead bodies were found in the well into which the Juda brothers were thrown on July 26. On the winch of the well there are bullet marks, and brown stains are visible on the coping. The man and five of the women were killed by bullets, the three others had probably fainted when they were thrown into the well. The only girl among the women, age eighteen, is undressed and perhaps was raped; her body is mutilated. The last one to be thrown down the well was Marthe Krameisen.

On August 9 the Gestapo of Bourges evacuates the premises. That same evening the militia of Saint-Amand leaves town. On August 11 the last Gestapo agents, who had arrived from Orléans in the meantime, abandon Bourges. On August 17 the prison doors finally open, restoring freedom to twenty-five women and nine children, survivors of the roundup of Saint-Amand.

EPILOGUE

Destinies

Bourges would be liberated on September 6; Saint-Amand, the first town to have staged an uprising, would be the last one liberated, on September 13, 1944. Instead of a liberation, it would be more fitting to speak straight out of a celebration, for there is not a single German soldier left in town. As of the night before, René Sadrin is no longer mayor of the town. He has been replaced by Lucien Maillaud, whom he himself replaced on January 15, 1941. Villatte, on the other hand, goes back to being subprefect, and this time it is official. Lalonnier's Popular Regiment of the Berry, the Surcouf commanded by Chaillaud, and Colonel Bertrand's First RI enter the town on September 13 and parade down the streets. The colonel delivers a speech in front of the monument to the dead, in the presence of Van Gaver's wife, president of the Saint-Amand Liberation Committee. Then they go to the place de la République, which just got its name back (the rue du Maréchal Pétain has in turn become rue Nationale), where the orators all take their turn at the rostrum. The new prefect, the new mayor, and the president of the CDL (Departmental Liberation Committee) express their emotion. In his speech the vice president of the Saint-Amand Liberation Committee, attorney André Damon, recalls the insurrection of June 6: "For our City, there will be Glory beyond measure for having won its freedom as early as June 6, the very day our allies landed, by forcibly removing its

Bastille, the symbol of the Tyranny that was suffocating it [is he referring to the militia mansion?]. For Saint-Amand will have once again [again?] been in the forefront of battle" (*La Voix républicaine*, 23 September 1944).

This is no time for reflection or nuances.

There is some rapid settling of scores, some militiamen or other "traitors" are shot to death without being tried or are beaten to death; some women are forced to have their heads shaved. But things fall quickly back into place, too quickly for some people. Men of power rapidly resume their positions, and yesterday's collaborators or indifferent citizens claim they resisted all along and gain privileges for themselves. Chaillaud, promoted to city councilman, proposes that a street in Saint-Amand be named for Van Gaver and another for Blanchard. The proposal is turned down. The former Vichy hostages form a committee, and through Théogène Chavaillon, now president of the National Front in Saint-Amand, they ask for "swift, implacable cleanup measures" after they observe the obvious inadequacy of the purge (*La Voix républicaine*, October 21, 1944). Their request does not result in any action.

In mid-September, Charles Krameisen appears at the Bourges police station and tells how he escaped a massacre. No one believes him; his story is muddled, and he speaks French badly. Not only that, twenty-five dead bodies would be visible. He insists, and other Jewish families report the disappearance of their loved ones. The Berry Committee for Remembrance and Gratitude takes his story seriously, and searches are organized. In mid-October the farm at Guerry and the wells are located. Some personal items that belonged to the women are retrieved from the first well. No longer is there any doubt that Krameisen's story is true. With great difficulty, thirty-six dead bodies are pulled from the wells, twenty-eight men and eight women. The bodies are transferred to Saint-Amand and buried on October 27.

The next day, October 28, a ceremony is organized for the repatriation of the eleven men in the Surcouf who were killed. Chaillaud gives a speech in which he justifies the uprising: "They understood that it had to be Frenchmen who liberated their homeland." "François," who has come to mark the occasion, follows him at the rostrum. He keeps trying to explain the torrent of blows suffered by the Surcouf in the Creuse: "Unfortunately, the traitor is not as rare a commodity in France as one would think. The Germans were meticulously informed of the location of all our units . . ." (*La Voix républicaine*, November 4, 1944). One has to wonder whether the Germans actually needed specific informers in order to know that there were maquisards in the forests of the Creuse and whether "François" is not just covering up his own responsibility in the resisters' delayed response to the news of the advance of the German columns.

Some maquisards join the French army and do battle at Royan and in Alsace. Others prefer to return to their civilian occupations. At the end of the war the deportees begin to reappear. Out of the sixty-one from the Surcouf, thirteen will not return, among them Lieutenant Le Quellec, the eloquent Champion, and Jean-Pierre May, who had saved his brother at La Croix de la Mine. The former deportees are rather shocked to see the extent to which nothing has changed. Business goes on as before; the same individuals regain their hold on the reins of power. A few of them have suddenly become rich, and people talk in veiled terms of misappropriations of funds parachuted in from London not long ago. When the resisters attend the celebrations of the Liberation, ritualized henceforth, they are stunned to find themselves face to face with some of their former adversaries, who are there to participate in the ceremonies as if nothing had happened. When he arrives with some comrades at the monument to the dead, Chaillaud orders them in a hushed tone, "Turn around, we're leaving, there are some people present who shouldn't be here."

One of the families of the executed militiamen sues for dam-

ages in order to bring about an investigation of the circumstances
of the death. Chaillaud and some others are questioned by the
criminal investigations officials, and they are afraid they will be in-
carcerated. Some of them throw away their Resistance member-
ship papers and decide never to think about it again. The investigation comes to a sudden end, however, and there is never any
trial. For his part, Lalonnier is accused of abusive requisitions and
is detained for several weeks at the central prison in Paris. But it
seems that in this case it is above all a question of a political squab-
ble: some people now fear the growing influence of the Communist Party and attempt to compromise its emblematic figures.
Lalonnier leaves prison entirely "clean."

Pierre-Marie Paoli, Joseph Lécussan, and Clément Marchand
are arrested, condemned, and shot to death in 1946. At the end of
the war, Francis Bout de l'An takes refuge in Italy, where he will
live for the remainder of his life; the rest of the family stays in
France. Auguste Vigier also emigrates, to Argentina, it seems.
Merdsche is condemned to death in absentia in 1950 by the court
of Lyons, which does not prevent him from practicing his occupations in Germany, first as a judge, then as an editor of judicial
publications. He has since retired.

René Sadrin harbors some bitterness for the rather cavalier
manner in which he was dismissed from the mayor's office in 1944.
However, he is also happy to withdraw from public affairs, to take
care of his sprained ankle, and compose his memoirs in peace and
quiet. Dr. Roques goes on to a fine political career, becoming the
(Gaullist) deputy for the district. Camille Guillemin and his wife,
who had a ninth child after the war, receive the Cognaq-Jay
medal, awarded to large families. For the most part, the widows of
the men killed in the summer of 1944 get married again, some to
veteran resisters, some to former police agents; yet others remain
forever faithful to the memory of their dead husbands.

After the war, Charles Krameisen files for naturalization, point-

ing out his ordeal under the Occupation. His application is accepted, and it is as a French citizen that he goes back to Lorraine.
But he finishes his life in a psychiatric hospital.

The destiny of Georges Chaillaud is a peculiar one. When he
is back at work in his prewar job, he is embittered by how quickly
people forget the rights and wrongs committed under the Occupation. He nevertheless participates in all of the anniversary celebrations in Saint-Amand. The speeches he gives, however, become increasingly bitter and more and more out of step with the
evolution of the country. On June 6, 1946, he complains of the
scant purging that followed the Liberation and promises, "Tomorrow we will struggle, all of us together, to prepare a new June
6, a June 6 of total victory" (*La Voix républicaine*, June 15, 1946).
At that time his message is the same as that of the Communists,
although Chaillaud is not one of them. The bases of his convictions are more personal. On June 6, 1947, his tone is even more
virulent. He denounces a France that has taken up its old con-
ciliatory practices, "a France smothering in paperwork and regulations." The return to civilian life ostensibly is not easy for him.
He continues, "We demand gallows, and not just for traitors, but
also for those who, as civil servants, failed to carry out the duties
of their offices. The battle goes on . . ." (*La Voix républicaine*, June
14, 1947). If a fight is going on at the time, it is certainly not one to
settle scores with former civil servants of the French State. Chaillaud lets himself go; he starts drinking. Does he regret the execution of the militiamen? He does not say so in the account of events
he gives to Delperrié de Bayac in 1967. But one day in 1968 he
comes by to say his good-byes to his Resistance comrades and tells
one of them, "I'm leaving on a long trip." Ten minutes later, he
kills himself with a revolver he had taken from the enemy during
the war.

Today most of the people in this story are deceased: Sadrin, Villatte, Delalande, and the others. The wells of Guerry now sit im-
posingly amid a verdant landscape, with the brambles removed

and the buildings restored. The veterans of the Surcouf, whose numbers are dwindling, continue to gather on anniversary dates, and they do not always manage to agree as to how a specific operation unfolded. They are known and respected in the region, although they see that the world around them is becoming less and less interested in them. They have the impression that soon there will no longer be anyone capable of understanding their adventure or establishing the truth about it.

A French Tragedy

In many respects, the story of the liberation of Saint-Amand is typical rather than exceptional, for one comes across many others like it in that summer of 1944. What makes it a special case are not its historical characteristics but rather what might be called its dramatic and ethical qualities.

By dramatic qualities I mean this: in real life many deeds are functions of pure chance and leave us with an impression of arbitrariness: "causes" often have no repercussions; "effects" spring out of nowhere. In this story it is just the opposite, many times over, for the actions are linked together, beckoning each other, responding to each other. Once the decision is made to take over the town (and given the characters present at the start, they could not have decided not to do so), it is as if everything were already programmed to happen: the imprisonment of the militiamen, the retreat to the bush, the taking of hostages in Vichy, their liberation, and even the roundup of the Jews and their murder at Guerry. Of course, this impression of fatality is in part an illusion imposed on us by hindsight. At the very moment that the action occurred there were choices to be made. All that would have been necessary to prevent the massacre at Guerry from taking place was that Vigier not be replaced by Lécussan. The fact remains, however, that the connecting force between episodes is great and that it creates a paradoxical and utterly tragic effect: the road to hell is paved with good intentions.

This interdependence of episodes is not only narrative; it extends as well to the moral value of the actions. Nothing is more common in real life than unrewarded good and unpunished evil. In this case, everything corresponds: good with good, evil with evil, even though the episode occurring second is not the effect of a cause but rather the symbolic counterpart of the first. The assassination of Thévenot, an unjustifiable act, gives rise in turn to the death of the women hostages. The execution of the militiamen, a regrettable action even though unavoidable, is immediately followed by the massacre of the Jews. The takeover of Saint-Amand on June 6, motivated by noble but politically questionable motives, leads to the tragic morning of July 19 a month and a half later, when the Surcouf Company is decimated. On the other hand, the efforts of the mediators, who seek only to save human lives, will meet with great success: their hostages are liberated, on both sides, and return home safe and sound.

On the ethical level, what is striking in this story is that its different characters deserve qualified judgments. This obviously does not apply to the victims. They—and I am thinking here first of those people put to death at the wells at Guerry—are exempt from any judgment whatsoever but arouse unlimited compassion. These particular deaths are different from the others. "There is no comparison between open battle and being snuffed out during the night. There is no comparison between the lot of a soldier and the lot of a hostage," wrote Saint-Exupéry in 1943 (344). There is an immense difference between those who die fighting because they choose to risk their lives and those who, as members of the civilian population, merely withstand the suffering, having done nothing to provoke it or to protect themselves from it. The difference is recognized in the courts as well. Whereas the members of the Surcouf died as a result of the war while trying to kill enemy soldiers (there is no crime in this, legally), the execution of civilian populations is a war crime, aggravated here by a crime against humanity, since it is not just any portion of the population that is singled out but rather those who have been declared less worthy of living than the others, in this case the Jews. Thus, in addition to the widespread cruelty that is characteristic of war, there is ignominy. The death of these Jews is a scandal because it punishes people for what they are, not for what they do.

Some of the victims of Guerry did engage in some forms of resistance. It is not due to these activities, however, that they were persecuted. The situation is somewhat different for those who died on June 8, at the time of the German repression. Some of them were killed simply because they happened to be at the wrong place at the wrong time. Others are true resisters but do not die in combat (their deaths are also war crimes even though they were not premeditated, as in the case of the wells at Guerry). Their fate is not only deadly, it is also fraught with a certain absurdity. With the passage of time, people try to attach a nobler meaning to each sacrifice. In 1969, Delperrié de Bayac, an otherwise decidedly critical writer, records this about an episode of June 8: "A small group remains in the rearguard. It is commanded by Second Lieutenant Sagnelonge, Blanchard's brother-in-law. . . . A brief encounter pits [the German forces] against some of Second Lieutenant Sagnelonge's men. . . . Captured by the Germans, Second Lieutenant Sagnelonge and the maquisard Girardhello are immediately shot to death" (2:99–100).

Likewise, Alain Rafesthain affirms in 1990, "At about 5:00 A.M., [the German soldiers] first clashed with Sagnelonge's men. Three of them . . . are captured and executed" (108). Yet Sagnelonge died following a misunderstanding, not while carrying out a mission. His death is moving; it is not necessary.

On the other hand, the other protagonists in our story are not pure victims. They act, make choices, enjoy their freedom, and exercise their will. It is therefore they who are subject to moral judgment.

Joseph Lécussan and his lieutenant are in great part responsible for the massacre at Guerry, for Lécussan takes the initiative for the roundup, and his lieutenants establish the lists and perform the arrests (the remaining guilt must be assigned to the Gestapo chiefs Merdsche and Hasse, complacent cogs in a criminal system). That they might have been acting while intoxicated most of the time is no excuse but leads us to ask: did they need to deaden their wits with alcohol to be capable of performing their misdeeds without any resistance from within themselves? Lécussan and his kind illustrate the disastrous consequences of a combination of factors. For one thing, they are convinced totalitarians (in this case, Fascists) for whom certain segments of the population are total enemies (Jews, Communists) and as such must be eliminated (and even so, the Communists could convert, but not the Jews, because the Jews constitute a "race"; among the victims at Guerry are some Jews who converted to Catholicism). For another thing, they are not content to profess their views in the abstract; they put them into practice. These are men of action for whom tangible proof is required to safeguard their honor, men who were raised in a spirit of masculine confrontation and domination.

Lécussan is not an anomaly, a raging sadist like the ones encountered in all wars, who would profit from circumstances to assuage his instincts. On the contrary, he is the logical product of a system. He is more consistent than the others, and it is they, the weak men, who are the anomalies. Lécussan shows where it can lead to consider life as a battle, to think that not all human beings are endowed with the same dignity. Therefore, his wrongdoing can continue to serve as a warning to us: no human group can allow itself to think it is immune to such bouts of violence.

Francis Bout de l'An is a more ambiguous figure even though he is a national leader of the militia, a convinced Fascist, and a member of the Waffen SS. Is he wrong to take hostages in Saint-Amand in order to free his wife, who is detained as a hostage? The taking of hostages is reprehensible in itself, for it denies the subject's responsibility and establishes a so-called guilt by association. Under the circumstances, however, Bout de l'An speaks the only language that he hopes will be understood; the same can be said for Vigier. How can he force the maquisards to release their hostages? By taking others himself, who are as dear to them as his wife is to him: their parents, their children, their brothers and sisters. The maquisards have not left him much choice. He respects the contract into which he has entered and even takes it one step further when he is no longer in a position of weakness: he frees all the hostages from Saint-Amand, including the ones who really did have a hand in the uprising and even the wives of the other resisters.

Despite this, Bout de l'An is clearly not above all reproach. First of all, his behavior with the hostages once they are transferred to Vichy is odious, in both the threats he makes to them and the torture he inflicts on them. Second, the responsibility is entirely his when he deliberately chooses Lécussan to handle the hostage matter and, beyond that, preside over the destinies of the inhabitants of Saint-Amand. He knows very well what kind of man he is dealing with. Even worse, it is precisely because of Lécussan's notorious brutality that Bout de l'An chooses the man. He is therefore equally responsible for what occurred at the wells at Guerry, and he cannot wash his hands of it, for by assigning Lécussan to that position, Bout de l'An made the massacre possible. Last and somewhat paradoxically, it is his conduct with respect to his own men that is shameful. Not only does he do nothing to free them, he seems even to give his approval to the maquisards to kill them. To him it seems like an appropriate punishment for their crime, which is not having known how to protect his wife. Like "François," Bout de l'An is ready to execute those among his troops who are poor fighters. This makes him equally responsible with Chaillaud for the death of his men, or even more so. Such narrow-mindedness is inhuman. But it fits well with the character, who prefers principles over people and who most likely would stop grieving for his wife if only he could emerge victorious from the conflict he faces against the maquisards. He is a small man, and the image that other people have of him is more important than a human life.

It must be said, however, that he is not the only one in this situation and that a "François" on the opposing side is hardly more praiseworthy. This does not mean that both the militia and the maquis must be dismissed on equal terms. There is a qualitative difference between the two, an irreducible asymmetry, that resides in their ideals, in totalitarianism versus democracy. But individual beings are more than just the ideology they serve, and in the maquis there are, in this respect, individuals who are no more worthy of respect than some militia members. In my opinion, such is the case of "François," with regard to his implication in the matter of the Saint-Amand hostages. He too thinks only of his image as a leader and a tough guy, he too sees existence as one big power struggle, and he too is ready to sacrifice human beings (the civilian population of Saint-Amand) for the benefit of his principles. It is only by the good fortune that allowed the mediators to meet directly with the resisters that "François" is spared the responsibility of a massacre and the annihilation of a town of ten thousand inhabitants. He and his lieutenants play with people's lives as if they did not weigh heavily in comparison with the lofty political objectives that he and his men serve (which, in reality, only disguise a pride and a vanity far from noble). Making a whole town experience losses and turmoil or putting sixty hostages in front of a firing squad does not seem to cause them any particular problem of conscience.

But there are not just men like "François" and "Roger" in the Resistance; there are also men like Blanchard and Van Gaver. These two central characters in our story become involved in several important actions that merit individual attention.

Why do they decide in favor of taking over the town? It has been shown that the underlying reason for this action, aside from the manipulations to which they may have been subjected, is the conviction that to safeguard national dignity the country's native sons must liberate the nation themselves. They are not seeking to be effective immediately, for they know that even without their intervention the Allies will eventually liberate France. Their objective is a matter not of military strategy but of group psychology. It is for the same reasons that in August 1944 the Parisians rise up instead of waiting for the regular troops to arrive; and after all, it is in the same spirit that on June 18, 1940, de Gaulle decided to resist rather than calmly wait for the Nazi defeat. Although today this type of sentiment is not part of the spirit of the times, it remains worthy of respect and praise. It is preferable that one's fate (also) be the product of one's will, that a person act as an autonomous subject. Through their action these Resistance fighters contribute to the creation of an image that the community as a whole will have of itself and that in turn will influence the behavior of each individual. They are thus working for the public good. It would have to be hoped nonetheless that the action's positive effect would not entail a decreased lucidity, fostering in the present case the illusion of complete autonomy. The Resistance actions are not insignificant, nor are they the whole answer; at the time, France was in no condition to liberate herself single-handedly.

But the acts that take place in the public sphere, such as taking over and occupying a town, cannot be judged exclusively in terms of the intentions that motivated them. As they say, political life is a matter not of the ethics of conviction but of the ethics of responsibility. Its manifestations are judged not in function of what precedes them but of what ensues, of their effects rather than their motivations. The criterion that allows each of these acts to be legitimized must therefore be as follows: in full knowledge of the facts, can I be sure that the good that should ensue from this will be greater than the bad that could come from it?

This same criterion must also be applied to actions that the adversary calls terrorist and that risk bringing about reprisals: are they

worth the cost? It is not that, out of principle, raids should be giv-
en up all together but that they not be carried out in those in-
stances where the expected benefits do not justify them. That is
why the execution of Thévenot on August 7 is unacceptable; at
the time its benefit is minimal, and the foreseeable negative effect
(the execution of ten hostages) is greater by far. It probably would
have been better to live with doubts about the "pseudo-maquisard" and let Thévenot save himself by going into hiding. The
hostages executed on August 8 would then have lived.

Taking over and occupying the town of Saint-Amand must be
judged by the same measure. Though justified from the perspective of an ethics of conviction (by the motivations that lead to it),
this action is not justified from the perspective of an ethics of responsibility, by its foreseeable consequences. The enemy forces
present are too out of proportion with the Resistance fighters, who
cannot hold "open towns." Whether they wanted to or not, the resisters leave the civilian population hostage: it is the resisters who
act, and the civilian population that suffers the consequences. The
just attitude is that of Guingouin, who refuses the directives of the
COMAC, not that of Van Gaver and Lalonnier, who are eager to
implement them.

After the attack on the mansion where the militiamen were
staying, the second important act by Van Gaver and Lalonnier is
the imprisonment of the militiamen and the taking of hostages
(Simone Bout de l'An and later the other women). In fact, the two
actions must be separated. After the surrender of the militiamen,
the Resistance fighters have a choice of three solutions: (1) shoot
them, as Lalonnier proposes; (2) release them; (3) keep them as
prisoners. But the first solution is excessive, and the second one is
absurd. These men just finished shooting at them, and if they let
them go free, they will immediately start shooting at them all over
again. Holding them prisoner is thus the right measure to take
even if it does carry some risk and obvious difficulties. Under the

circumstances this choice by Van Gaver and Blanchard was the best one possible.

It is true that things turned out badly. For this reason, after the war's end, the execution of the militiamen gave rise to various commentaries. Chaillaud himself, who was never one to shy away from the facts, presented them in another light in his speech given on June 6, 1946, in Saint-Amand: "The militiamen are captured, [he says, recalling the events of June 6, 1944], a couple of them are executed, the others will be later on" (*La Voix républicaine*, June 15, 1946). As in other contemporary documents, the execution is depicted here as the result of a quasi-judicial decision and no longer as an unavoidable deed called for by circumstances. If, on the other hand, putting two militiamen to death on June 6 can be presented as an act of war, it is obviously not the same for the killing of the thirteen others, who were more like prisoners of war.

In 1976 the veteran chief of the FTP, Marcel Cherrier, in collaboration with a historian, Michel Pigenet, wrote a book that expresses the Communist point of view of the Resistance in the Cher, *Combattants de la liberté*. Their presentation of the execution is the following: "The militiamen are hanged in retaliation for the crimes committed by their friends" (p. 139). The authors of this sentence embrace the logic, or rather the illogic, of retaliation. Whether the "friends" in question be militiamen or German forces, it is impossible to understand how one group can be held responsible for the crimes committed by the others.

Conversely, certain accounts filed in the departmental archives emphasize the promise made to the militiamen by Van Gaver at the time of their surrender and attribute responsibility for the execution to "François," who was called head of the FTP for the occasion. "François," who had tremendous loathing for the FTP, could have given such an order, but it happens that on July 20 all contact between Chaillaud and "François" was cut off.

In volume 8 of his "in-depth history of the French under the

Occupation," *Joies et douleurs du peuple libéré* (1988), Henri Amouroux cites Chaillaud's account as reported by Delperrié de Bayac and adds this commentary: "Between the hanged men of Tulle and the hanged men of the Coires farm, there is, in the executioners, a difference of motivation, but not of method" (p. 405). There is something very excessive in comparing the reprisals of Tulle, where the German army hangs ninety-nine hostages to avenge the death of sixty-nine soldiers the night before, to the execution of the thirteen militiamen by the maquisards at bay. Unless one takes "method" to mean strictly the hanging process and unless one therefore suggests that all the hangings in the world have the same meaning, one cannot in good faith equate a measure of arbitrary retaliation with executing prisoners because it became impossible to keep them.

For the death of the militiamen, which is not justified either as the "execution" of an imaginary sentence or of an order from on high, or as retaliation for other contemporary crimes, is understandable as a woeful necessity in its own particular context. Chaillaud had the impression that he did not really have any choice; he reasoned that if we wanted to preserve his own men, he had to sacrifice the others. It is the situation itself that is tragic because it forces him and his comrades to kill those who, even in their own eyes, do not necessarily deserve to die. The maquisards who participated in this tragedy still live it as one even to this day. Some of them simply refuse to talk about it ("Even if I knew something, I wouldn't tell it to you. . . . Not all truth is good for telling, even fifty years later . . ."), others cannot bring it up without getting teary-eyed ("I do not agree. I cannot accept that. I do not like to tell about it. Painful. Painful. Painful"), and even those who believe that the action was unavoidable recognize that they have regrets ("There was nothing else that could have been done; it was them or us, but it was not done with a happy heart").

The execution of the militiamen was experienced as a tragic necessity, but it is not a matter of justice. Some of these men had perhaps committed crimes, had killed or, what amounts to the same thing, denounced Resistance fighters, Communists, and Jews to the Gestapo. But not a single one of them was judged, and they did not die in combat. Instead of being men executed by reason of a guilty verdict, they too were victims: victims of the fierce civil war that Frenchmen waged against Frenchmen in that summer of 1944. It is improper to continue to heap opprobrium on them, to surround them with silence (their names, even their exact number, are still not well known); these dead men also deserve a sepulcher.

Let us now return to the situation of the women and of Simone Bout de l'An in particular. It is totally different from that of the militiamen; the women cannot be considered prisoners in the same way since they were not fighters as the men were. Moreover, they were treated differently from the start: they are hostages, that is, a means of acting upon the adversary, an exchange value, and thus human beings transformed into instruments of action. During the night of June 7–8, Van Gaver and Blanchard were perfectly capable of taking with them the militia fighters and releasing the women. By following the course of action they chose, they assumed that the end justifies the means and thereby acted in the same way as their enemies. In this way they recall the dilemma raised by François Mauriac in 1943 in Le Cahier noir, concerning the fight waged against the adversary: "In order to stand up to him, does he not condemn us to become just like him? Even in defeat, will he not force us to die inside ourselves only to be recreated in his own horrible likeness?" (47).

Moreover, kidnapping Simone Bout de l'An, making her a hostage, would in no way prevent German retaliation. Indeed, at a second stage it is precisely the kidnapping that risked causing new reprisals, since the sixty-four hostages would be kept in prison as revenge for this kidnapping. Sorcerer's apprentices, the leaders of the Resistance in Saint-Amand unleashed forces that they could no longer control. In situations like this it must be expected that there will be elements that will escape all control; the unforeseeable must be foreseen. Things could have turned out even worse: if all of the interlocutors had been as intransigent as Lécussan and "François," the kidnapping of Simone would have produced another seventy dead. It was only the obstinate insistence of the mediators that allowed this additional carnage to be avoided.

If Van Gaver and Blanchard committed an error in all this, they did have the courage to admit it and make amends for it instead of trying to protect their pride. When the time came, they did everything in their power to save the Saint-Amand hostages, on the one hand, and their own hostages on the other. It is not their fault if the exchange is carried out to the exclusion of the men.

Finally, there is the last act of their lives: their heroic deaths. Daniel Blanchard, killed at age twenty-five, leaves behind the image of an admirable human being. He took on his responsibilities until the very end. It is thanks to him that the Resistance fighters of Saint-Amand were where they were; it is he who would be on the front line to defend them. He is a true fighter, in whom strength nevertheless did not stiffen to become hardheartedness; he is a hero who aspired not to heroism but to doing good. He is also a man who believed in the redemptive virtues of sacrifice and proved the genuineness of his beliefs by practicing what he preached, by sacrificing himself so that his homeland would live.

There remains the civilian population. But harbored within it are two attitudes that must be distinguished. The first one consists of waiting passively for fate to strike its blows; of taking refuge in oneself, in resignation, or indifference; of hoping that better times will come; of even taking occasional advantage of the misfortune of others. Conversely, the second attitude suggests that, while remaining a member of this peace-loving civilian population, one take action, and facing extreme circumstances and prompted by concern for others, one take personal initiatives. One thereby refuses, as do the resisters, merely to wait for things to fall back into place and for the wind to change direction; one refuses always to obey and to be transformed into a serf for an indefinite period. Yet despite all this, one does not seek to change the social order.

The people acting in the latter way in this story are first of all Mayor Sadrin, who took the initiative to mediate and proposed himself as a hostage in place of the others. They are the untiring Delalande and Villatte, who traveled the roads hither and yon, exposing themselves to the bullets of German soldiers, the roadblocks of the militia, and the ambushes of the maquisards and who wore themselves out trying to reorient the stubborn pride and intransigence of all the parties involved. They are Riche and Jarrige, who helped them by ignoring their fatigue and taking risks. They are Msgr. Lefebvre, who proposed himself as a hostage and did all that he possibly could to prevent the execution of others. They are Briandet and Bodain, who preferred to remain prisoners rather than have their comrades risk death. They are the peasant Camille Guillemin, who, upon discovering the wild-eyed Charles Krameisen, found the right words, "I will keep you." Bernard Delalande deserves special mention. Not only did he think nothing of going to tremendous lengths to save the hostages in Vichy, but later he was the only one to try to arrange the release of the Jews victimized in the roundup. After the Liberation he would sometimes come and testify in favor of certain militiamen menaced at that time by collective resentment. Should we add to this enumeration Marthe Krameisen and the other two Jewish mothers who preferred to die like childless women rather than endanger the lives of their little ones?

It is not that the political agenda of these individuals, these antiheroic heroes, is superior to any other (as that of the maquisards is, compared to that of the militiamen); it is just that for them, human beings, their lives and their dignity are superior to political agendas, whatever they might be. They act as advocates for those in need of help, and they intercede on behalf of the potential victims. This does not dispense with the necessity of having an agenda but brings to it a necessary complement without which all politics risks becoming inhuman.

It could be said that, in the course of these tragic events, two types of moral practice operated side by side and even overlapped.

The first one was a morality of sacrifice. What it implied, even if the idea surfaces only rarely in people's consciousness, is that redemption demands sacrifice, that the death of the individual is beneficial, indeed it is indispensable, to the survival of the community. This morality has its sinister version, which boils down to selecting a scapegoat (thus, Lécussan wanted to redeem his homeland by purging it of what he saw as a stain, the Jews and the Communists), and a heroic version, which consists of offering oneself on the sacrificial altar (thus, Blanchard assumed his death so that his beautiful homeland would live, as if the spirit of the nation could blossom only if nurtured with the blood of the individual). As contrary in spirit as these two attitudes may be, they hold in common the conviction that sacrifice is necessary.

In the face of such a conviction, a few other characters who also are strangers to indifference, apathy, and resignation adopted what could be called a morality of risk, a morality devoid both of the sacred and of violence. By proposing themselves as hostages, by devoting themselves to being mediators, by hiding the persecuted, these human beings took calculated risks in which death played no role. Their actions were in no way extraordinary (that is why they could then return to everyday life without too much difficulty): rather than exceptional courage, they demanded a faith in man—you must have some faith in man if you are going to start acting all over again, day after day—and an intimate awareness of the community of men. Each one of them understood that he could not live happily if misfortune struck those beside him.

In the great moments of history, heroes are necessary to the homeland. But it is throughout the course of their existence that human communities need carriers of these humble, everyday virtues. And it is their presence in the tragic history of the liberation of Saint-Amand that gives us a few glimmers of hope.

BIBLIOGRAPHY

Published Works Concerning the Events at Saint-Amand

Autissier, Albert. "La libération de Saint-Amand." *Le Berry républicain*, June 6, 7, 8, 1984. Summarizes and quotes various eyewitness accounts, including that of François Villatte, June 8, 1972.

Les Bandes de Picardie. Paris: Librairie Lamarre, 1946. An account of their resistance actions by the members of the First RI, including Colonel Bertrand.

Chavaillon, Théogène. "La libération de Saint-Amand et les journées tragiques de juin 1944." *La Voix républicaine*, (Saint-Amand) January 5, 1946 (reprinted in *Le Berry républicain*, September 12 and 15, 1964). The story of one of the hostages in Vichy.

Cherrier, Marcel, and Michel Pigenet. *Combattants de la liberté*. Paris: Editions sociales, 1976. Told from the same perspective as that of Granger, upon whom the authors rely heavily, but more complete.

De La Barre de Nanteuil (General). *Historique des unités combattantes de la Résistance (1940–1944), Cher*. Château de Vincennes: Ministère de la Défense, 1975. Statistics with commentary.

Delalande, Bernard. *De la milice au maquis*. Saint-Amand: Author, 1945. A most scrupulous account—the author made use of Sadrin's notes—containing the list of Vichy's hostages.

Delperrié de Bayac, Jacques. *Histoire de la milice*. 2 vols. Paris: Fayard, 1969. Reprint, Verviers: Marabout, 1985. (Page citations are to the reprint edition.) The first comprehensive account of events; contains previously undisclosed eyewitness accounts by Georges Chaillaud, Francis Bout de l'An, and several other militia members. A wealth of information on the militia.

Granger, L. *Quatre Ans de lutte pour la liberté: Les communistes au combat*. Sancerre: Société coopérative des ouvriers d'imprimerie, 1946.

An account centered around the resistance activities of the FTP, told from a Communist point of view.

Guédin-Dreyfus, Georgette. *Résistance Indre et vallée du Cher.* Paris: Editions sociales, 1970. Told from the Communists' point of view. Eyewitness accounts by Fernand Sochet, Mignaton, and "Roger," whose version of events is entirely false.

Lyonnet, Jean. *L'Affaire Paoli*, 2d ed. Nevers: Chassaing, 1965. (First edition 1964; continually republished ever since). Written in 1946 by the committing magistrate who worked on the case, based primarily on Paoli's version of events and that of certain survivors of the roundup of the Jews in Saint-Amand.

Parrotin, Marc. *Le Temps des maquis.* Aubusson: Imprimerie d'Aubusson, 1981. Considers resistance in the Creuse from a point of view that is hostile toward "François."

Perrot, Paul-Daniel. *La Surcouf du Boischaut.* Bourges: Amicale des anciens du maquis du Cher, 1980. By one of the survivors in the Surcouf, deported to Germany; contains the list of deportees.

Rafesthain, Alain. *1944 . . . Et le Cher fut libéré.* Bourges: Royer, 1990. The most complete available history of resistance in the Cher region in 1944 (the same author has published several other works devoted to resistance in the Cher); uses all published eyewitness accounts plus some unpublished memoirs.

Sadrin, René. "Souvenirs d'un maire." In Tzvetan Todorov, *Une tragédie française, été 1944: Scènes de guerre civile.* Paris: Editions du Seuil, 1994. Notes written in 1944–45 and reworked in 1956.

La Tragédie de Guerry près Bourges, Cher. Bourges: Berry Committee for Remembrance and Gratitude, 1945. A commemorative booklet giving a detailed account, eyewitness reports, photographs, a list of the victims. Reprinted with additional information in 1995.

General Works

Amdoroux, H. *La Grande Histoire des Français sous l'Occupation.* Vol. 8, *Joies et Douleurs du peuple libéré.* Paris: Robert Laffont, 1988.

Aron, R. *Histoire de la Libération de la France.* Paris: Fayard, 1959.

Azéma, J.-P. *De Munich à la Libération, 1938–1944.* Vol. 14 of *Nouvelle Histoire de la France contemporaine.* Paris: Le Seuil, 1979.

Azéma, J.-P., and F. Bédarida, eds. *La France des années noires.* Vol. 2. Paris: Editions du Seuil, 1993.

Courtois, St. *Le PCF dans la guerre.* Paris: Ramsay, 1980.

Guingouin, G. *Quatre Ans de lutte sur le sol limousin*. Paris: Hachette, 1974.

Kriegel-Valrimont, M. *La Libération*. Paris: Editions de Minuit, 1964.

La Libération de la France. Paris: Editions du CNRS, 1976.

Mauriac, F. *Le cahier noir*. Paris: Editions de Minuit, 1985.

Nicault, N. *Le Berry dans la guerre*. Le Coteau: Horvath, 1986.

Noguères, H., et al. *Histoire de la résistance en France de 1940 à 1945*. Vol. 9. Geneva: Famot, 1982.

Saint-Exupéry, A. de. "Lettre à un ôtage." In *Ecrits de guerre*. Paris: Gallimard, 1984.

Newspapers

Before the Liberation
Le Nouvelliste du Centre, (Saint-Amand)
La Dépêche du Berry; (Bourges)

After the Liberation
La Voix républicaine (Saint-Amand, Communist)
Le Berry républicain (Bourges); see in particular a series of commemorative articles published in September 1964 under the title "Twenty Years Afterward."

Unpublished Material

Viollet, Jacqueline. "Au service de l'Allemagne, la collaboration dans le Cher." Thesis for the Diplôme d'Etudes avancées, Paris, 1990, on file at the Departmental Archives of the Cher. A very precise, accurate study; a useful guide for the departmental archives.

Interviews, conducted in 1992–93, of Emile Augonnet, Andrée Berjamin, Jeannine Blanchard, François Briandet, Hervé Evenat, Georges Kiejman, Adolphe Lauroy, Lucien Louis, Pierre Sadrin (the former deportee), Pierre Sadrin (the nephew of the former mayor), Jean Vannier.

Archives

Departmental Archives
11 F 15 (documents of the Berry Committee for Remembrance and Gratitude)

M. 7018 (general intelligence reports)
M. 7247 (police reports)
M. 7298 (Jewish affairs)
Z. 1524 (militia)
Z. 1555 (subprefecture reports)
755 W 1 and 2 (the Paoli affair)
755 W 25 (the Marchand affair)

National Archives
72 AJ 111 (resistance, liberation of Saint-Amand)